THE EVOLUTION
OF DARWIN'S RELIGIOUS V.

Charles Darwin in 1880
Photograph courtesy of the Syndics
of the University of Cambridge Library

THE EVOLUTION OF DARWIN'S RELIGIOUS VIEWS

NABPR Special Studies Series, Number 10

by
Frank Burch Brown

MⳐP MERCER UNIVERSITY PRESS, Macon, Georgia 31207

ISBN 0-86554-239-2

The paper used in this publication meets the minimum requirements
of American National Standard for Information Sciences—
Permanence of Paper for Printed Library Materials, ANSI Z39.48-1984.

Library of Congress Cataloging-in-Publication Data
Burch Brown, Frank.
    The evolution of Darwin's religious views.

    (NABPR special studies series; no. 10)
    Includes index.
    1. Darwin, Charles, 1809-1882—Views on religion.
2. Religion—History—19th century.   I. Title.
II. Series.
BL48.D355B87   1986   200'.92'4   86-19978
ISBN 0-86554-239-2   (alk. paper)

TABLE OF CONTENTS

For Ralph Auldon Brown

PREFACE

When Charles Darwin claimed that his views on God and religion were of no consequence to anyone but himself, he was clearly uttering an opinion that was not widely shared. But he generally acted as though it were true, seldom addressing explicitly religious and theological issues. One of my primary aims in this study of Darwin's religious views is to show how these views actually were of "consequence"—to Darwin first, and then to others. In order to do that, I must interpret what these views were and how they compared with Christian orthodoxy, especially the kind represented by natural theologies of Darwin's time and specifically that of William Paley.

Because the very idea of a natural theology is now relatively unfamiliar outside certain circles and is misrepresented by a number of writers interpreting Darwin's religious thought and science, it will be helpful to clarify the concept at the outset. Technically, natural theology is that form of theology that entails the use of reason (perhaps in conjunction with other "natural" endowments, such as the capacity for sensing and feeling) to attain some kind of knowledge of God, and to do so without the aid of special revelation. Thus natural theology is concerned with demonstrating what one can know about God simply by virtue of being a thoughtful and perceptive human. Because it may utilize formal arguments for the existence of God that make no reference whatsoever to what we ordinarily think of as "nature"—to the cosmos and the creatures that inhabit it—natural theology has no direct and intrinsic connection with natural phenomena or with natural science.

In practice, however, natural theology has rarely ignored nature altogether. Particularly in England and North America during the eighteenth and early nineteenth centuries, natural theologians constantly looked to the natural world for evidences of God's existence and attributes. In this respect, at least, these theologians were not far removed from the mainstream of Christian orthodoxy in other times and places. Virtually all Christian theology has affirmed with the Psalms that the heavens declare the glory of God and has accepted the statement in the book of Romans that "ever since the creation of the world [God's] invisible nature, namely, his eternal power and deity, has been clearly perceived in the things that have been made'' (Rom. 1:18, RSV).

It is this basic affirmation that Darwin found difficult to uphold in view of his theory of evolution by natural selection. Precisely why this was so, and how he and others dealt with the consequent crisis in their theistic beliefs, is the subject of much of the following study.

I am grateful to Roger Ariew, James C. Livingston, Duncan M. Porter, and Elizabeth Struthers Malbon for reading various versions of this study and offering not only encouragement but also helpful criticisms that I have tried to take into account. I am also indebted to Anita Malebranche of the Carol M. Newman Library, Virginia Polytechnic Institute and State University, for assistance in securing materials essential to my research, and to Barbara Scheid for patiently typing last-minute revisions of the manuscript. Timely support for an earlier form of the project came from John C. Greene. My wife, Carol Burch-Brown, provided both support and valuable comments from the very beginning. My father—to whom this monograph is dedicated—played what was probably the most important though least obvious role, having done more than anyone else to stimulate my interest in science and in relations between science and religion.

A major portion of this study first appeared in the *Journal of the History of Biology* under the title ''The Evolution of Darwin's Theism.'' Permission to reprint that material in revised and expanded form has been kindly granted by the editor of the journal and by its publisher, D. Reidel Publishing Company.

INTRODUCTION

The photographs taken of Charles Darwin late in life (indeed, from his fifties on) make him seem a kind of sage, venerable and enigmatic. It is an impression no doubt created partly by the imposing figure and by the copious, untrimmed beard hiding much of his face.[1] But while Darwin seems to have relished looking sage,[2] he did not fancy himself particularly wise in metaphysics or religion. In these matters he was deeply and designedly reticent. Nevertheless, his legacy undeniably has been religious as well as scientific. Although he lived in relative seclusion and was by nature a private person, Darwin was also a public figure and a representative Victorian—an illustrious ''modern'' trying at a crucial moment in history to make emotional and intellectual sense of the world. His views on God and religion are thus naturally of special interest, not only to scientists and religion scholars but also to the public at large.[3]

It is unfortunate, therefore, that the various pictures we have been given of Darwin's life and thought are less subtle and suggestive with regard to his religious attitudes than the photographs are with regard to his general de-

---

[1]Perhaps in Darwin's case the Victorian fascination with physiognomy was justified. One contemporary spoke of Darwin's character as having been ''palpably written on his face.'' See Ralph Colp, Jr., *To Be an Invalid: The Illness of Charles Darwin* (Chicago: University of Chicago Press, 1977), caption to plate 4.

[2]See R. B. Freeman, *Charles Darwin: A Companion* (Folkestone, Eng.: Dawson, 1978) 66-67.

[3]It is plain that Darwin's own ideas of religion and God remain interesting to a wide range of people involved in the study or practice of religion. Witness such popular interpretations (and partial misinterpretations) as William E. Phipps, ''Darwin, the Scientific Creationist,'' *The Christian Century* (14-21 September 1983): 809-11. The special fascination with, and credence given to, the whole range of ideas of any major figure such as Darwin—even when the ideas extend beyond the realm of that person's expertise—undoubtedly has to do partly with the phenomenon one Darwin scholar refers to as the ''lure of biography.'' See Janet Browne, ''Essay Review: New Developments in Darwin Studies?,'' *Journal of the History of Biology* 15 (1982): 275-80; quotation on 279.

meanor. It may be true that, as Michael Ruse says, "Darwin simply cared less about religion than many other men."[4] But Darwin's religious concerns were in fact more pervasive, and his theological reflections more persistent and complex, than Ruse and a number of others have recognized. Until recently, scholars have on the whole been content to reiterate the thesis Maurice Mandelbaum set forth in 1958—namely, that Darwin moved more or less steadily from almost total orthodoxy in his youth, through deistic heterodoxy following the *Beagle* voyage, to an eventually complete agnosticism in the years after the *Origin*.[5] That this view must now be judged inadequate is evident from the material brought to light by researchers during the past two and a half decades: the unexpurgated autobiography, voluminous correspondence, notebooks, the "long version" of the *Origin of Species,* and so on.

The present study is not the first attempt to draw on such material to reassess the nature and development of Darwin's religious ideas and the vicissitudes of his theism.[6] Recent discussions of the overt and covert influence of theology on Darwin's science have been particularly enlightening.[7] Mandelbaum's article was the last effort to be truly synoptic, however, and the consequent need for a thorough reexamination of Darwin's religious views has been noted for some time by scholars in both science and religion.[8] In the absence of any systematic ordering and interpretation of the evidence, it is no

---

[4]Michael Ruse, *The Darwinian Revolution* (Chicago: University of Chicago Press, 1979) 182.

[5]Maurice Mandelbaum, "Darwin's Religious Views," *Journal of the History of Ideas* 19 (1958): 363-78.

[6]The most pertinent previous studies will be cited or discussed here in relation to particular questions regarding Darwin's life and thought. For a perceptive and useful overview of relevant publications, see James C. Livingston, "Darwin, Darwinism, and Theology: Recent Studies," *Religious Studies Review* 8 (1982): 105-16. One important book in Darwin studies that is neither cited by Livingston nor discussed at length here is *The Darwinian Heritage,* ed. David Kohn (Princeton NJ: Princeton University Press, 1985). Due to its late publication, the book became available after this monograph was already in the publisher's hands. The volume's more than one thousand pages contain much of value to Darwin scholars but relatively little that has a direct bearing on the present topic. The material that is of special relevance is referred to in several subsequent notes.

[7]For one of the finest and most recent of these discussions, see John Hedley Brooke, "The Relations Between Darwin's Science and his Religion," in *Darwinism and Divinity: Essays on Evolution and Religious Belief,* ed. John Durant (Oxford: Basil Blackwell, 1985). Brooke includes an excellent bibliography. Because so many authors now have addressed ably the question of how Darwin's theological background may have shaped the formation of his scientific theories, I have chosen to concentrate here on the nature and transformation of Darwin's religious and theological ideas themselves.

[8]See Livingston, "Darwin, Darwinism, and Theology," and Dov Ospovat, "God and Natural Selection: The Darwinian Idea of Design," *J. Hist. Biol.* 15 (1980): 169-94; esp. 170. Although Livingston does not overtly stress in his article the need for an overall reassessment of Darwin's religious beliefs, he has done so in conversation, and the article makes the need abundantly clear.

wonder that, in Peter Bowler's words, "a major disagreement still remains concerning Darwin's religious views and the rapidity with which he threw off—[or whether he ever did completely throw off]—the traditional belief that nature is designed by a benevolent God."[9] To this observation it must be added that almost all of the existing studies have erred in underestimating the degree to which a human being—and especially a Victorian—can hold apparently incompatible beliefs and can vacillate time and again between them. Accordingly, scholars have failed to appreciate fully the extent and importance of the ambivalence that characterized Darwin's theology at every stage of its evolution, and particularly in its final phase of an intermittent and largely "agnostic" theism. It is to this last, lengthy phase and its unresolved tensions that we shall return after examining the overall development and near-demise of Darwin's theistic beliefs.

---

[9]Peter J. Bowler, *Evolution: The History of an Idea* (Berkeley: University of California Press, 1984) 145. James R. Moore, in contrast to Bowler, seems to think that the question of Darwin's religious beliefs is now settled despite, in his opinion, the lack of a truly "disinterested interpretation" of Darwin's religious life. Jacques Roger, commenting on Moore's views, obviously disagrees; whereas Moore says that Darwin was a "muddled theist to the end," Roger regards the mature Darwin as simply an agnostic. Neither analyzes the tensions in Darwin's religious thought or tries to specify the reasons for those tensions. See James R. Moore, "Darwin of Down: The Evolutionist as Squarson-Naturalist," and Jacques Roger, "Darwinism Today," in Kohn, ed., *Darwinian Heritage*, 435-81, 813-23.

CHAPTER 1

A PECULIAR ORTHODOXY

The dogmatic content and religious commitment of Darwin's early Christianity have been the subject of speculation and debate. But there is no disputing that in 1831, when Darwin set out on his five-year voyage around the world as a naturalist aboard HMS *Beagle,* he was not only an avowedly orthodox member of the Church of England but also a prospective clergyman, having studied theology and classics while earning a B.A. at Cambridge. In fact, one of the arguments Darwin's uncle Josiah Wedgwood had used to persuade Dr. Robert Darwin that his twenty-two-year-old son should be allowed to embark was that the enterprise would not in the future be "in any degree disrespectable to his character as a Clergyman," the pursuit of natural history being "very suitable" for one of that profession.[1]

This last point is something Charles had known very well when, some four years before, he had abandoned medical studies at Edinburgh and, on his father's advice, had begun to think of preparing for the life of a "country clergyman."[2] The possibility of uniting a parish ministry with the study of natural science had soon been further impressed on Darwin's mind by his close association at Cambridge with the Reverend Professor John Stevens Henslow. An eminent geologist and botanist, Henslow was a deeply religious clergyman—one so orthodox that, according to Darwin, he professed "he should be grieved if a single word of the Thirty-nine Articles were altered."[3] It was Henslow, of course, who was later to recommend Darwin for the post on the *Beagle* and whom Darwin would ultimately eulogize, saying, "I fully be-

---

[1]Quoted in Charles Darwin, *The Life and Letters of Charles Darwin,* ed. Francis Darwin, 2 vols. (New York: D. Appleton, 1896) 1:172 (hereafter cited as *LLD*).

[2]Charles Darwin, *The Autobiography of Charles Darwin, 1809-1882,* ed. Nora Barlow (New York: Harcourt, Brace, 1958) 56-57. Hereafter all citations to *Autobiography* indicate above work by Darwin.

[3]Ibid., 64-65.

lieve a better man . . . never walked this earth.''[4] In his *Autobiography* Darwin notes that, like Henslow, he himself did not at this time ''in the least doubt the strict and literal truth of every word in the Bible.''[5]

The accord between religion and science that Darwin saw so immediately manifest in the person and career of Henslow was likewise apparent to him in the writings of William Paley. At Cambridge the required mastery of Paley's *Principles of Moral and Political Philosophy* (1785) and *View of the Evidences of Christianity* (1794), together with Darwin's voluntary and delighted study of Paley's *Natural Theology* (1802), marked the high point of his education. Taking Paley's premises on trust, Darwin was ''charmed and convinced by the long line of argumentation,''[6] a great deal of it relying heavily on arguments from design. In his *Natural Theology* Paley reasoned that, just as one can deduce when coming upon a watch that ''its several parts are framed and put together for a purpose,'' so one can deduce from the even more marvelous and intricately designed works of nature—and particularly from anatomical features such as the eye—that they must have been produced by a providential and intelligent Creator.[7] ''Design must have had a designer. That designer must have been a person. That person is God.''[8]

As is well known, the premises of Paley's arguments were of a kind that had already been challenged by David Hume. But Darwin did not read Hume until after the *Beagle* voyage and Paley himself deemed Hume worthy of only passing mention in his *Natural Theology*.[9] So it is not surprising that, in Darwin's thinking from this point on, Paley's work represented the best that orthodoxy could do rationally to justify both theism and religious belief as a whole. For the time being, moreover, Paley's natural theology provided Darwin with an exalted—albeit circumscribed—conception of science as a uniquely valuable means of discovering and verifying the universal workings of a Supreme Intelligence, wonderfully powerful and good. The scientist or anyone else following Paley's train of thought would be led, in Paley's view, to regard ''the phenomena of nature with a constant reference to a supreme intelligent Author. . . . The world thenceforth becomes a temple, and life it-

---

[4]Charles Darwin, *Darwin and Henslow: The Growth of an Idea, Letters 1831-1860*, ed. Nora Barlow (Berkeley: University of California Press, 1967) 19.

[5]*Autobiography*, 57.

[6]Ibid., 59.

[7]William Paley, *Natural Theology* (unabridged editions) chaps. 1-3, 14.

[8]Ibid., chap. 23.

[9]In the introduction to his readily accessible abridged edition of Paley's *Natural Theology*, Frederick Ferré writes: ''Amazing as it may appear, our author does not even refer to Hume by name'' (William Paley, *Natural Theology: Selections* [Indianapolis: Bobbs-Merrill, 1963] xi). This, however, is not true; Paley refers once to Hume and the *Dialogues Concerning Natural Religion* near the end of chap. 26, in a section Ferré omits.

self one continued act of adoration.''[10] It is this kind of "enlightened" orthodox theism that Darwin was at this time more than happy to embrace.[11]

What can easily be forgotten is how unlikely it is that Darwin's orthodoxy per se was ever deeply and securely rooted. Yet the odds definitely were against his ever being, as Mandelbaum claims, "thoroughly orthodox."[12] One notes, for instance, that Darwin's family was by no means conventionally religious. His famous grandfather, Erasmus Darwin, who died in the year Paley's *Natural Theology* appeared, was an evolutionary deist. His notorious *Zoonomia* expressed a philosophy that Coleridge once characterized as "State of Nature or the Orang Outang theology of the human race, substituted for the first chapters of the Book of Genesis."[13] It was later a source of pride for Charles himself that *Zoonomia* was, in his words, "honoured by the Pope by being placed on the 'Index Expurgatorius.' ''[14]

Although Charles's father, Robert, was less outspoken than his grandfather, Charles remembered him after his death as a "free thinker in religious matters" and indicated that his connection with the Church of England was what Charles's own had become—that is, strictly "nominal."[15] The father's unconventional religious attitudes are perhaps most clearly revealed in his remark to Charles, shortly before the latter's marriage in 1839 to Emma Wedgwood, that a certain woman (a sister-in-law) was surely a skeptic because, in his opinion, "so clear-sighted a woman could not be a believer."[16] Dr. Darwin went on to poke fun at another woman who, suspecting the doctor's "unorthodoxy," tried to convert him by arguing: "Doctor, I know that sugar is sweet in my mouth, and I know that my Redeemer liveth."[17] Robert Darwin's urging his son to study for a parish ministry reflects worldly wisdom

---

[10]Paley, *Natural Theology*, chap. 27.

[11]Edward Manier, in his important study of influences on the youthful Darwin, downplays Paley's influence except with respect to his style of argumentation and the nature of his theodicy, which entailed the principle of chance. But Manier slights and skews Darwin's autobiographical testimony and does not do justice to the shrewdness and subtlety of Paley's own thought. In addition, Manier is misleading in calling Paley a deist; for Paley affirmed what the deists characteristically denied, namely, divine revelation of truths inaccessible to natural reason. See *The Young Darwin and his Cultural Circle* (Dordrecht, Holland: D. Reidel, 1978) 69-75, 164-66; and Paley, *Natural Theology*, chap. 27.

[12]Mandelbaum, "Darwin's Religious Views," *Journal of the History of Ideas* 19 (1958): 363.

[13]Quoted in Nora Barlow, "Charles Darwin and his Grandfather," Appendix, *Autobiography*, 151.

[14]Quoted in Howard E. Gruber, *Darwin on Man: A Psychological Study of Scientific Creativity*, 2d ed. (Chicago: University of Chicago Press, 1981) 68. Originally published as book 1 of Howard E. Gruber and Paul H. Barrett, *Darwin on Man* (New York: E. P. Dutton, 1974).

[15]*LLD*, 2:356.

[16]*Autobiography*, 96.

[17]Ibid.

more than piety. By Charles's own admission, his father had been afraid his
son would squander his days and inheritance in the sporting life Charles loved
so passionately.[18] If Charles became a clergyman, it might at least save him
from dissolution and prodigality.

It is impossible to know just how far Robert's heterodoxy went or how much
of it was communicated to Charles in his youth. We do know that the father's
influence was immense and that Charles's elder brother, Erasmus, leaned
strongly toward atheism for much of his life. As a little boy, Charles had at-
tended a Unitarian chapel with his mother and older sisters. After his mother
died when Charles was eight, he went to Anglican services.[19]

In any case, his beliefs may never have been entirely orthodox when judged
by Church of England standards. While Charles was seventeen and a student
at Edinburgh University, his elder sister Caroline told him in a letter that she
hoped he read the Bible—thus implying there was some reason to doubt that
he did—and closed her remarks on religion with a revealing comment: "I
suppose you do not feel prepared yet to take the sacrament." A second letter
of Caroline's dated less than a month later suggests that Darwin quickly re-
assured her that he had indeed been studying the Bible and had a special lik-
ing for the Gospel of John and the Epistle of James. It does not indicate that
Darwin had tried to reassure Caroline with regard to his apparent lack of read-
iness to take the sacrament.[20]

Such hesitancy accords with Charles's doctrinal uncertainties when he first
entertained his father's proposal that he become a clergyman. "I asked for
some time to consider," he recalls in his autobiography, "as from what little
I had heard and thought on the subject I had scruples about declaring my belief in all the dogmas of the Church of England."[21] To be sure, the *Autobiography* tells us that, after studying a few books in divinity, Charles soon
"persuaded" himself that "our Creed must be fully accepted." But the words
"persuaded" and "must be" are ambiguous, leaving open the possibility that
pragmatic considerations were a significant factor, as they were for many
nineteenth-century divines.[22] The *Autobiography* interprets his youthful stance
as mainly reflecting that he had had "no wish to dispute any dogma," even
though he could not understand or find intelligible that to which he was prepared to give assent.[23] This reluctance openly to reject or attack religion was
to be a lifelong trait.

---

[18]Ibid., 56-57. Cf. Peter Brent, *Charles Darwin: "A Man of Enlarged Curiosity"* (New York:
Harper & Row, 1981) 71-72.

[19]*Autobiography,* 22.

[20]Charles Darwin, *The Correspondence of Charles Darwin,* ed. Frederick Burkhardt and
Sydney Smith (Cambridge: Cambridge University Press, 1985) 1:36, 41.

[21]*Autobiography,* 56-57.

[22]See James C. Livingston, *The Ethics of Belief: An Essay on the Victorian Religious Conscience.* AAR Studies in Religion 9 (Missoula MT: Scholars Press, 1974) 1-16.

[23]*Autobiography,* 9.

Darwin's doubts about his spiritual fitness for a religious vocation surfaced once again in the midst of his studies at Cambridge. In conversation with J. M. Herbert, a friend likewise studying to be a clergyman, Darwin spoke of misgivings. As Herbert recalls, "We had an earnest conversation about going into Holy Orders; and I remember his asking me, with reference to the question put by the Bishop in the ordination service, 'Do you trust that you are inwardly moved by the Holy Spirit, etc.,' whether I could answer in the affirmative, and on my saying I could not, he said, 'Neither can I, and therefore I cannot take orders.' "[24] This was in 1829, just two years before Darwin's graduation. The doubts must have subsided enough for Darwin to continue preparing for ordination, and their importance could easily be exaggerated. It was at about this same time that Darwin wrote a letter of consolation to a religious cousin in which he spoke of the "pure and holy comfort" the Bible affords in the face of death.[25] Still, it is probable that Darwin's uncertainty about "going into Holy Orders" never entirely disappeared. Meanwhile his keen interest in natural history had not flagged in the least. On the contrary, hoping to emulate his idol Humboldt, he was already planning to make a scientific voyage to the Canary Islands when the *Beagle* post became available. Darwin's studies in divinity were thus anything but single-minded, and his commitment to the institutions and beliefs of orthodox Christianity may never have been wholehearted.

---

[24]*LLD*, 1:147. It is possible that Francis Darwin attributes this quotation to the wrong Herbert. James R. Moore writes that J. M. Herbert "had not read divinity at Cambridge; it was Herbert's cousin Whitley and [Darwin's] own cousin Fox, who were establishing themselves as clergymen." Moore, "Darwin of Down," 448 in Kohn, ed., *Darwinian Heritage,*.

[25]*LLD*, 1:153.

CHAPTER 2

A THREATENED THEISM

As we have noted, Darwin boarded the *Beagle* intending, however vaguely, to become a clergyman. He quoted the Bible to the ship's officers, treating it "as an unanswerable authority on some point of morality";[1] he planned to read the Greek New Testament on Sundays;[2] and he is known to have spoken up in defense of the Church of England.[3] A year after embarking he wrote home saying he still had "a distant prospect of a very quiet parsonage" that he could see "even through a grove of Palms."[4] Yet he was sounding more tentative half a year later when he wrote his clergyman cousin W. D. Fox: "I hope my wanderings will not unfit me for a quiet life, & that in some future day, I may be fortunate enough to be qualified to become, like you a country Clergyman." The gradual demise of Darwin's aspirations toward clerical life is charted in remaining letters. In September of 1833 Charles's younger sister Catherine wrote prophetically, "I have great fears how far you will stand the quiet clerical life you used to say you would return to." Writing to Fox again in 1835, Darwin declared outright, "I do not know what will become of me," though he said he still envied the life of a clergyman, which he described as "a type of all that is respectable & happy" to "*a person fit to take the of-*

---

[1] *Autobiography*, 85.

[2] Charles Darwin, *Charles Darwin's Diary of the Voyage of H.M.S. "Beagle,"* ed. Nora Barlow (Cambridge: Cambridge University Press) 14. One should not assume from this that Darwin was an astute student of the Bible. It was not until 1861 that he realized (upon being informed) that the statement that the world was created in 4004 B.C. came not from the text of the Bible itself but from marginal notes derived from the work of Archbishop Ussher. See Charles Darwin, *More Letters of Charles Darwin,* ed. Francis Darwin, 2 vols. (New York: D. Appleton, 1903) 2:31 (hereafter cited as *MLD*).

[3] *Charles Darwin's Diary*, 243-44. All references unless otherwise indicated refer to works of Charles Darwin.

[4] To this his brother Erasmus replied, "I am sorry to see in your last letter that you still look forward to the horrid little parsonage in the desert."*Correspondence of Charles Darwin,* 1:227, 259.

fice.'' Just before Charles's voyage was over, his sister Susan wrote, ''Papa & we often cogitate over the fire what you will do when you return, as I fear there are but small hopes of your still going into the Church.''[5] Darwin's plans for a clerical vocation thus may have been somewhat slow to die the ''natural death'' he recalls in the *Autobiography.*[6] But die they did, along with any semblance of orthodox Christianity.

Howard Gruber has argued that, because Darwin ended the voyage a totally committed scientist, after beginning it with aspirations toward a ''quiet parsonage,'' his religious views must have been very much in flux all the while, carrying him rapidly toward agnosticism.[7] It will be seen that this is unlikely. To be sure, Darwin's references to religion during the *Beagle* years were fewer than one might reasonably expect from a clergyman-to-be. The correspondence between Darwin and Henslow scarcely mentions reli-

---

[5]Ibid., 286, 333, 460 (emphasis added), 489. For one interpretation of possible changes in Darwin's religious views during this time see Sandra Herbert, ''The Place of Man in the Development of Darwin's Theory of Transmutation, Part 1, ''*J. Hist. Biol.* 70 (1974): 216-58. See also n. 7 below.

[6]*Autobiography,* 57. James R. Moore argues that, even after Darwin returned to England, he still intended to become a country parson. According to Moore, the main reason Darwin had felt possibly ''unfit'' for the role of clergyman while on the *Beagle* voyage was that he became acutely aware that he lacked any prospect for the wife he would be expected to have if he were to be a clergyman. Temporarily, love of nature came to substitute for the love of a woman, which necessarily made the idea of a parish seem remote. Although this interpretation may contain a grain of truth, it ignores the family's views of the matter and Charles's failure to express, even on his return, any eagerness actually to become a clergyman. Moore goes on to observe that Darwin eventually married, ended up at Down—in what was once a parsonage—and took up some of the social duties that a clergyman could also have been expected to perform. But this certainly does not prove that Darwin envisioned himself the naturalist parson-squire (or squarson) that Moore depicts him as having in some sense become. It only means that Darwin had always liked the general ''life-style'' of country clergymen, which is no secret. See Moore, ''Darwin of Down,'' in *The Darwinian Heritage,* ed. David Kohn (Princeton NJ: Princeton University Press, 1985) esp. 440, 446-49, 464-73.

[7]Charles Darwin, *Metaphysics, Materialism, and the Evolution of Mind: Early Writings of Charles Darwin,* transcribed and annotated by Paul H. Barrett, commentary by Howard E. Gruber (Chicago: University of Chicago Press, Phoenix Edition, 1980) 176. Originally published in slightly different form as book 2 of Howard E. Gruber and Paul H. Barrett, *Darwin on Man* (New York: E. P. Dutton, 1974). Sandra Herbert thinks that the changes in Darwin's religious views during his voyage were minimal but depicts his original decision to become a clergyman as totally a matter of complying with his father's wishes. Oddly, she interprets Darwin's *Autobiography* as saying that *during* the voyage itself Darwin turned against the Old Testament on moral and scientific grounds. But, as almost all other commentators have recognized, Darwin's statement that ''I had gradually come, *by this time,* to see that the Old Testament . . . was no more to be trusted than the sacred books of the Hindoos'' alludes to the period of time he has just referred to as ''these two years'' involving much religious reflection—years he specifically dates as those immediately after his voyage, from 2 October 1836 to 29 January 1839. This is consistent with his claim, in the same passage, that while on board the *Beagle* he was ''quite orthodox.'' See Herbert, ''Place of Man, Part I,'' 217-20, 232-33; *Autobiography,* 82, 85 (emphasis added).

gion or any other topic outside science. For his part, the Reverend Henslow, always inquisitive and informative about things botanical or geological, never alluded to the prospect of Darwin's coming home to a parish ministry; indeed he complained that his own parish abounded in "poor, & small farmers who leave every thing to the parson without attempting to assist him."[8] Darwin, in turn, was virtually silent about God and religion.

Yet this is not a sufficient basis for thinking that Darwin's Christianity—or Henslow's either—had drastically altered. Darwin's preoccupation with science and quiet abandonment of the idea of a parsonage signifies nothing so much as that Darwin had found his true vocation. If he had really rejected Christianity in the process, he would never have written so favorably and at such length of the work of the missionaries in Tahiti, which he observed not long before returning to England.[9] The observations recorded in his diary were mirrored in a letter to Henslow:

> Tahiti is a most charming spot. . . . It is moreover admirable to behold what the Missionaries both here [Australia] & at New Zealand have effected. —I firmly believe they are good men working for the sake of a good cause. I much suspect that those who have abused or sneered at the Missionaries, have generally been such as were not very anxious to find the Natives moral & intelligent beings.[10]

It is true that Darwin was here praising the ethical and educational work of the missionaries rather than their evangelistic efforts. Later he would praise such work in equally ethnocentric terms, even after avowing himself an agnostic.[11] But Darwin specifically stated in the *Beagle Diary* that, in his opinion, "the state of morality & *religion*" among Tahitians influenced by Christian missionaries was "creditable."[12]

More significant with respect to Darwin's religious attitudes during the voyage, the *Autobiography* mentions (and the *Diary* confirms) that he experienced religious sentiments "whilst standing in the midst of the grandeur of a Brazilian forest"—feelings of "wonder, admiration, and devotion which fill and elevate the mind."[13] According to the *Autobiography*, these "higher feelings" were the sort that had already led him to the "firm conviction of the existence of God, and of the immortality of the soul."[14] He also continued to think in terms of natural theology, as when he argued that the deaths of

---

[8]*Darwin and Henslow*, 90.

[9]*Charles Darwin's Diary*, 352-73.

[10]*Darwin and Henslow*, 114.

[11]*LLD*, 2:308.

[12]*Charles Darwin's Diary*, 355 (emphasis added). Cf. Robert FitzRoy and Charles Darwin, "A Letter, Containing Remarks on the Moral State of Tahiti, New Zealand, etc.," *South African Christian Recorder* 2 (1836): 221-38. Reprinted in *The Collected Papers of Charles Darwin*, ed. Paul H. Barrett (Chicago: University of Chicago Press, 1977) 1:19-38.

[13]*Autobiography*, 91; cf. *Charles Darwin's Diary*, 56.

[14]*Autobiography*, 91.

species in certain epochs must be followed by the birth of new ones, since otherwise the number of the world's inhabitants would vary greatly, violating the "fitness the Author of Nature" established.[15] Aboard the *Beagle*, therefore, Darwin cannot have been abandoning very rapidly his religion or his belief in God.

At the same time, it cannot be denied that, both before and after Darwin read Charles Lyell's *Principles of Geology* (1830-1833) while aboard the *Beagle*, his theology was being unsettled, and not only in ways directly correlated with his turning from a form of geological catastrophism toward Lyell's uniformitarian theories. In early diary notes Darwin showed himself capable of being baffled that the world's design is as it is: "Many of [the world's] creatures, so low in the scale of nature, are most exquisite in their forms & rich colours. It creates a feeling of wonder that so much beauty should be apparently created for such little purpose."[16] Much later, only nine months before returning to England, Darwin entered in his diary some theological musings having to do with the differences between the strange animals he had been observing in New South Wales and the animals he had seen in the rest of the world. After speculating about what an "unbeliever" would conclude—namely, that "surely two distinct Creators must have been at work"— he observed that a "Lion-Ant" (ant lion) he could see nearby belonged to the same genus as the geographically remote European kind. This confirmed for him that "one hand has surely worked throughout the universe," though perhaps "a geologist" would further suggest that "the periods of Creation have been distinct & remote the one from the other; that the Creator rested in his labor."[17] Darwin's 1839 version of the *Beagle Journal* included this passage but omitted the reference to the "Creator," whereas the 1845 version said nothing even of the "hand" at work in the universe, having relegated the remarks on the insect to a footnote.[18] A change was under way.

The years immediately following the *Beagle* voyage did in truth bring a far-reaching transformation in Darwin's religious as well as scientific thought. We know from Darwin's *Red Notebook* that, by 1837 at the latest, he was convinced of the mutability of species; his subsequent reading of Malthus in 1838 led him to conceive of natural selection as the means.[19] In that same year Darwin made the following entry in his *Journal:* "All September read a good deal on many subjects: thought much upon religion. Beginning of Oc-

---

[15]Quoted in Herbert, "The Place of Man, Part 1," 233.

[16]*Charles Darwin's Diary*, 23.

[17]Ibid., 383.

[18]See Howard E. Gruber, *Darwin on Man: A Psychological Study of Scientific Creativity*, 2d ed. (Chicago: University of Chicago Press, 1981) 295.

[19]See Charles Darwin, *The Red Notebook of Charles Darwin*, ed. with introduction and notes by Sandra Herbert, *Bulletin of the British Museum (Natural History)* Historical Series 7 (1980): esp. 8n.

tober ditto.''[20] The *Autobiography* concurs, asserting that between 1836 and 1839 he was "led to think much about religion."[21]

As to what he was thinking, the notebooks of the period, along with the uncensored version of the *Autobiography,* give many tantalizing clues.[22] We learn that Darwin was reading Hume on epistemology and religion, as well as pondering at least secondary literature on the positivist Auguste Comte. Simultaneously he was developing an increasingly materialist theory of mind and emotion. Upon coming across an anonymous review of Comte's *Cours de philosophie positive,*[23] Darwin was particularly taken with Comte's thesis that every branch of science progresses through three stages: the theological, the metaphysical, and the lawful.[24] "Zoology itself is now purely theological,''[25] Darwin remarked, meaning that zoologists still saw the providential hand of God intervening in the natural order. With Comte, Darwin rejected this theological state of current science. He had already, in fact, set aside the notion of Divine "interposition" and, hence, of special creation.[26] The vehement attacks on special creation found in his private "Essay on Theology and Natural Selection" from about the same time reveal the extent to which that notion had become scientifically repugnant to him.[27]

Whether Darwin could go so far as to agree with Comte that "all real science stands in radical and necessary opposition to all theology" is another question. The theological essay just mentioned (actually a commentary on John Macculloch's *Proofs and Illustrations of the Attributes of God* [1837]) made no attempt to deny that a deity designed the basic structure and laws of the "Great System" of the universe; what it denied was that explanations of specific events and structures in terms of the will of the deity can count as genuine explanations. Their explanatory value is doubtful, Darwin said, be-

---

[20]Charles Darwin, *Darwin's Journal*, ed. Gavin de Beer, *Bull. Brit. Mus. (Nat. Hist.)* Hist. Ser. 2 (1959): 8.

[21]*Autobiography,* 85.

[22]See Peter Vorzimmer, "The Darwin Reading Notebooks (1838-1860)," *J. Hist. Biol.* 10 (1977): 107-52.

[23]Anon., "Review of *Cours de philosophie positive* by Auguste Comte," *Edinburgh Review* 67 (1838): 145-62. The review, which was actually by Sir David Brewster, a Scottish "natural philosopher," is discussed at length in Sylvan S. Schweber, "The Origin of the *Origin* Revisited," *J. Hist. Biol.* 10 (1977): 229-316.

[24]*LLD,* 1:266. For Darwin on Comte, see "M" notebook, 69-70; 72-73, 81, 135-36; "N" notebook, 12; "Old and Useless Notes" (hereafter cited as OUN) 25, all published in *Early Writings of Darwin* (with original pagination indicated), ed. Barrett and Gruber. See also Gruber's comment on Darwin's response to Comte, 72.

[25]"N" notebook, 12.

[26]Charles Darwin, "Transmutation Notebook B," 101; quoted in Barrett and Gruber, *Early Writings of Darwin,* 185.

[27]Charles Darwin, "Essay on Theology and Natural Selection," (complete) in Barrett and Gruber, *Early Writings of Darwin,* 154-62.

cause they have nothing to do with natural law and predictability: "We know nothing of the will of the Deity, how it acts & whether constant or inconstant."[28] Significantly, the review of Comte that Darwin had read asserted against Comte that "the argument for design remains unshaken" and reaffirmed the necessity of "an all-directing mind."[29] On this opinion Darwin made no comment in either notes or letters.[30] The whole issue was, for him, highly charged. After reading the review he was "very much struck by an intense headache" from having had to "think deeply."[31] Presumably, if Darwin was of a mind to accept the reviewer's claims at all, it could now only be by confining the act and plan of God to the moment of aboriginal creation, leaving the rest to natural laws.

There are indications that even this remote role for God had begun to be questioned by Darwin, along with traditional views of revelation, religious experience, and Christian ethics. Whereas he had earlier considered certain feelings of a moral and religious nature to be evidence for the existence of God, his pursuit of a naturalistic or materialistic account of emotion and mind in the various notebooks of 1837-1840 entailed treating such feelings as animal in their origin.[32] Darwin speculated that material causes (experienced as "motives") could account for the "great effect" sometimes produced when a person hears the Bible for the first time.[33] Similarly, he considered it "an argument for materialism that cold water brings on suddenly in head, a frame of mind, analogous to those feelings, which may be considered as truly spiritual."[34] The "Golden Rule" he saw as explicable on grounds of survival value and instinct.[35] Where our behavior is evil, this too he could ascribe to our purely natural and animal inheritance: "Our descent, then, is the origin of our evil passions!!—The Devil under form of Baboon is our grandfather!"[36] As for human happiness, Darwin contended that it derives from doing good and from intellectual cultivation, though the latter (to his chagrin) is hardly mentioned in the New Testament. He dissented from what he took to be the New Testament's emphasis on future life and present self-mortification.[37] Finally, Darwin was inclined to reject the notion of free will, voicing

---

[28]Ibid., 5 (original pagination).

[29]Brewster, "Review," 245.

[30]Later, though for different reasons, Darwin applauded T. H. Huxley's attacks on Comte and positivism. See *LLD*, 2:328; *MLD*, 1:313, 382.

[31]"M" notebook, 81.

[32]Ibid., passim; "OUN," 7, 25-30.

[33]"OUN," 25.

[34]"M" notebook, 19.

[35]Ibid., 150-51; cf. Charles Darwin, "Moral Sense," in *The Descent of Man*, 2d ed., rev. (New York: D. Appleton, 1896) 97-127.

[36]"M" notebook, 122-23.

[37]Ibid., 118-22.

a suspicion that our so-called freedom actually arises from "fixed laws of organization" and that, as a consequence, no one deserves either credit or blame for anything. Such a view, he acknowledged, "would make a man a predestinarian of a new kind, because he would tend to be an atheist"—though he would also be humble and strive to do good so as "to improve his organization" for the sake of his children and to set an example to others, most of whom would continue to share the generally beneficial delusion of freedom.[38]

Acknowledging the almost universal belief in higher powers, gods, or God, Darwin was inclined to attribute it not to reasonable reflection but to instinctive response (a thesis he also found in Hume),[39] or else to a confusion between our sense of what we ought to do and our urge to postulate a necessary cause for why we should do it.[40] In any case, Darwin proposed that the idea of a God has a strictly material source: "—love of deity [is the] effect of organization, oh you materialist!"[41]

It is easy to see why scholars such as Michael Ghiselin, Edward Manier, Howard Gruber, and Sylvan Schweber have concluded that by or during this time Darwin ceased to be a theist. Gruber confidently asserts that Darwin became "a confirmed agnostic, probably sometime about 1840,"[42] and Schweber is still more emphatic, claiming that "by 1839 Darwin was certainly an agnostic (and possibly an atheist)."[43] Plainly we cannot accept without serious qualification the recurrently popular theory that Darwin remained a committed theist (or "evolutionary deist") throughout all the years prior to the completion of the *Origin of Species* (1859).[44]

---

[38]Ibid., 69-74; "OUN," 26-28.

[39]"N" notebook, 4, 101; "OUN," 11b. For an account of Hume's real but limited influence on Darwin, see William B. Huntley, "David Hume and Charles Darwin," *J. Hist. Ideas* 33 (1972): 457-70.

[40]"M" notebook, 151.

[41]"Transmutation Notebook C," 166.

[42]Barrett and Gruber, *Early Writings of Darwin,* 176. Sandra Herbert, while less committal in her opinions about Darwin's precise stance vis-à-vis the viability of a nonreligious or "neutral" natural theology, sensibly deduces that Darwin's "gradual disaffection from Christianity was well under way by this time," though this did not thereby make him an atheist. See "The Place of Man in the Development of Darwin's Theory of Transmutation, Part II," *J. Hist. Biol.* 10 (1977): 155-227; quotation on 201-202. Michael T. Ghiselin, by contrast, is essentially in agreement with Gruber. See "The Individual in the Darwinian Revolution," *New Literary History* 3 (1971): 113-34; esp. 122.

[43]Schweber, "Origin of the *Origin,*" 233. Manier is more cautious, suggesting that we should not term Darwin a "theist" at this point and yet insisting that he did not fit the categories "deist," "positivist," "atheist," or "agnostic" either, having a closer affinity for a Wordsworthian immanentism centered on the themes of love, struggle, meaningful chance, and hope. See Manier, *The Young Darwin and his Cultural Circle* (Dordrecht, Holland: D. Reidel, 1978) 89-96, 166-67, 195-96.

[44]This theory, advanced by Mandelbaum in 1958, has recently been further elaborated or

The notebooks are fragmentary and cryptic enough, however, to be open to differing interpretations. One cannot dismiss Neal Gillespie's contrary thesis that "Darwin's materialism [was] compatible in his mind with theism" and "represented no interest in a thoroughgoing atheistic philosophical or metaphysical materialism."[45] Dov Ospovat gives a similar assessment when he writes, "Darwin's 'materialistic' speculations on the origin of the idea of God offer no support to the argument that Darwin was an agnostic or atheist when he indulged in them."[46] Although these counterclaims cannot themselves be accepted at face value, they do rest on some important evidence that must be taken into account. For example, it does seem to be the case that Darwin was not prepared to take the metaphysical stance of declaring that matter in motion is the ultimate reality. A somewhat circumscribed notion of materialism is implicit in a letter in which he stated: "By materialism I mean, merely the intimate connection of kind of thought with form of brain. —Like kind of attraction with nature of element."[47] It may also be true that, as Gillespie and Ospovat both contend, materialism of some kind was, from Darwin's point of view, at least theoretically compatible with some kind of theism. Thus, even when thinking in materialistic and deterministic terms, Darwin could entertain the thought of a "Creator . . . governing by laws"[48] and could be intrigued that Sir Thomas Browne saw the determining will of the Deity

---

reiterated by a number of distinguished scholars, including Michael Ruse (*The Darwinian Revolution*, [Chicago: University of Chicago Press, 1979] 181; Neal Gillespie (*Darwin and Creation*, [Chicago: University of Chicago Press, 1979] 138-39); James R. Moore (*The Post-Darwinian Controversies* [Cambridge: Cambridge University Press, 1979] 314-26, 346-48); John C. Greene (*Science, Ideology, and World View* [Berkeley: University of California Press, 1981] 140, 153); and Dov Ospovat (*The Development of Darwin's Theory: Natural History, Natural Theology, and Natural Selection, 1838-1859* [Cambridge: Cambridge University Press, 1981] 60-86). Ruse appears simply not to be familiar with the evidence against his interpretation. Gillespie's research is meticulous, but he misses the import of key passages and appears to be unable to conceive that Darwin could later become *more* theistic for a time; it goes against his view of scientific progress. Moore acknowledges that Darwin saw why Comte himself was atheistic; but Moore does not perceive that this in any way disturbed Darwin's own theism. Greene explicitly allies himself with Gillespie, and implicitly with Moore, but is not entirely explicit about his reasons; he seems to assume that since Darwin was clearly an "evolutionary deist" at the time he was writing *Natural Selection,* he must have been no less so in earlier years. (See also John C. Greene, "Reflections on the Progress of Darwin Studies," *J. Hist. Biol.* 8 [1975]: 243-73; esp. 246-47.) Ospovat, familiar with the work of the others, provides valuable insights but almost willfully ignores the tenor of doubt and criticism in the very passages he cites in support of the view that Darwin was still unshaken in his theism while writing his notebooks of the mid to late 1830s.

[45]Gillespie, *Darwin and Creation,* 139.

[46]Ospovat, "God and Natural Selection: The Darwinian Idea of Design," *J. Hist. Biol.* 15 (1980): 183.

[47]Quoted in Gillespie, *Darwin and Creation,* 139.

[48]"M" notebook, 154 (excised passage).

behind apparently "chance" events and actions.[49] Darwin might have been thinking of the determinative act of God as the original creation of nature's thenceforth fixed and reliable laws. If so, this thinking found its corollary in the "M" notebook, where Darwin wrote of the mistake philosophers make when they say "the innate knowledge of [the] creator has been implanted in us . . . by a *separate act* of God" and not naturally by God's "most magnificent laws, which we profane in thinking not capable to produce every effect of every kind which surrounds us."[50] Although the emphasis in these passages is on natural laws rather than on God, it is true that the deity is still visible on the horizon.

All of this, hypothetically, leaves room for God. Yet, as we have seen, the notebooks and other material also plainly show that Darwin himself felt considerable tension between his materialistic scientific views and genuine theism, not to mention orthodox Christianity. Certainly, for him, nature had ceased to be the temple envisioned by Paley. In a letter written only a few years later to his botanist friend Joseph Hooker, Darwin at last made known his "presumptuous" theory of the mutability of species, and he did so with the comment that he felt as though he was "confessing a murder."[51] The tone is difficult to assess but the anxiety is hard to miss, as is the possibility that the implied victim of the "murder" was the God of orthodox theism. In the late 1830s, moreover, Darwin never unambiguously and forthrightly endorsed a theistic interpretation of the world order, whereas he did remark that his line of thought tended toward atheism. When he read atheistic or skeptical authors like Comte and Hume, he did so with keen interest and without criticizing their suspicions of religion or their incredulity toward God.[52] At the very least, then, Darwin's theism was undergoing a crisis, and it seems altogether probable that between 1836 and 1840 Darwin sometimes found that he himself did actually "tend to be an atheist."[53]

This is not to say, however, what Gruber, Schweber, and others have said—namely, that Darwin was from this point on a "confirmed agnostic" whose position was essentially that of an atheist who happened to be undogmatic in temperament. Darwin's use of materialist theories was primarily intended to eliminate not God as such but the twin possibilities of divinely revealed truth

---

[49]Ibid., 126.

[50]Ibid., 136 (emphasis added).

[51]*MLD,* 1:40-41.

[52]Darwin did at one point seem to object to Comte's attributing the laws of nature to "chance"; but the passage is extremely cryptic and he certainly did not go on to say that he himself regarded the laws a result of designing Providence. See "OUN," 25.

[53]See "M" notebook, 74.

and miraculous intervention,[54] both of which struck him as undermining the integrity and coherence of science. His subsequent scientific writings, letters, and autobiographical statements suggest, moreover, that in the 1840s Darwin drew back from his tendencies toward atheism and for at least two decades adopted a tentative and minimal sort of theism in accord with his sense of an intelligent purpose behind the marvels of the universe.

---

[54]See Ospovat, *The Development of Darwin's Theory*, 68.

CHAPTER 3

A THEOLOGY
WITHOUT RELIGION

Darwin is reported to have commented, late in life, that he had not given up Christianity until he was forty—that is, until about 1849, or thirteen years after the *Beagle* docked at Falmouth, England, and a decade before the publication of the *Origin of Species*.[1] As we have seen, there was an earlier phase in which he regarded many of the basic tenets of Christianity as highly questionable. It was near the end of this phase, in 1838, that Darwin was engaged to Emma Wedgwood and was cautioned carefully by his father to conceal from her his doubts, lest he bring on great misery.[2] Darwin's later assertion that he did not give up Christianity for another ten years is therefore curious, to say the least, and cannot be taken to mean that he had not come *near* to giving it up or that his Christianity was at all orthodox. Yet it indicates that the earlier ''crisis of faith'' did not completely and permanently undermine his theistic beliefs. It suggests, too, that we must take Darwin seriously when he says in his *Autobiography:* ''I was very unwilling to give up my belief [in Christianity]. . . . Thus disbelief crept over me at a very slow rate.''[3]

How, then, did his eventual outright rejection of Christianity come about, and why? In 1873, Darwin responded to a question regarding his independence of judgment by remarking that he ''gave up common religious belief [that is, in Christianity] almost independently,'' due to his own reflections.[4] The fundamental reasons for Darwin's abandoning ''common religious belief'' are related, no doubt, to the ideas expressed in the early notebooks; but

---

[1]The sole source for this information appears to be Edward Aveling's pamphlet *The Religious Views of Charles Darwin* (London: Freethought, 1883) 5.

[2]*Autobiography,* 95.

[3]Ibid., 86-87.

[4]*LLD,* 2:357.

they are formally stated in his *Autobiography*. According to Darwin's account, in the years after the *Beagle* voyage he gradually came to regard the Old Testament images of a revengeful and tyrannical God as abhorrent and to look on its marvelous sagas as no truer than the tales in "Hindoo" scriptures "or the beliefs of any barbarian" (a strong statement, given Darwin's low opinion of "barbarians"). The notion that God could permit a revelation of divine truth to be associated with such primitive and untrustworthy forms seemed to him "utterly incredible." As for New Testament miracles—which Paley had treated as basic evidence of the truth of Christianity[5]—the advance of science had, for Darwin, made them unbelievable and had shown just how ignorant and credulous the people of that former day were. In addition, Darwin recalls, he could no longer ignore the many "inconsistencies and inaccuracies" of the Gospels. This meant that, however "beautiful" the morality of the New Testament, the Christian scripture, in his eyes, no longer had the status of revelation. Darwin stresses in the *Autobiography* that this conclusion was not one he arrived at quickly; ever the scientist, he tried hard to think of evidence that could somehow validate Christianity and demonstrate the truth of its sacred texts—but all to no avail. His disbelief was "at last complete." He felt no distress at this, in the end, and never doubted his conclusions. Indeed, it was soon hard for him to imagine how anyone could even wish Christianity were true, since it would condemn such people as his father, brother, and best friends to everlasting punishment—a "damnable doctrine."[6] Darwin's objections to Christianity thus were based on epistemological, historical, and moral grounds.

What was left when Darwin's Christian belief was gone was a kind of natural theology, an evolutionary theism, that would have struck Paley as most *un*natural, since it was severed not only from Christianity in particular but also from any real sympathy with religion as a whole. This minimal philosophical theology undeniably figured in work leading up to the *Origin*. In the preliminary "Sketch of 1842," for example, Darwin wrote that the operation of secondary laws without divine interference is a result of a more basic law of nature "impressed on matter by the Creator," a creator Darwin explicitly referred to as omniscient and highly exalted in power.[7] The "Essay of 1844" likewise conceives of a creator or a god-like being essential to the workings of nature, although not necessarily perfectly omniscient or omnipotent:

Let us now suppose a Being with penetration sufficient to perceive differences in the outer and innermost organization quite imperceptible to man, and with forethought extending over future centuries to watch with unerring care and se-

---

[5]See William Paley, "Preparatory Considerations" and part 1 of *A View of the Evidences of Christianity* (1794).

[6]*Autobiography*, 85-87.

[7]Charles Darwin, *The Foundations of the Origin of Species: Two Essays Written in 1842 and 1844*, ed. Francis Darwin (Cambridge: Cambridge University Press, 1909) 51-52.

lect for any object the offspring of an organism produced under the foregoing circumstances; I can see no conceivable reason why he could not form a new race . . . adapted to new ends.[8]

Later, Darwin used theistic language in *Natural Selection*—the large, incomplete volume Darwin began to convert into "digest" form in June of 1858 when he heard news of Wallace's similar evolutionary theory. No doubt remembering Paley, Darwin admitted that one could not reasonably think such an "inimitable" organ as the eye could be perfected by natural selection if eyes were necessarily made in the way humans make telescopes; but this inference he thought presumptuous: "Have we any right to suppose that the Creator works by the same means as man?"[9] He explained that by "nature" he meant "the laws ordained by God to govern the universe" and more than hinted at divine agency when he theorized that, in accordance with these natural laws, all animals and plants have descended from a few ancestral types or "some one form" into which "life was first breathed."[10] Darwin even paraphrased the New Testament with reference to the great future in store for those races that manage to survive: "In the great scheme of nature, to that which has much, much will be given."[11] That such language was not casual or perfunctory is corroborated by the *Autobiography*, where Darwin says that when he was at work on the *Origin of the Species* (presumably in the 1850s), he was a theist who had strongly in mind the conclusion that this "immense and wonderful universe" must have a First Cause with an intelligent mind in some degree analogous to that of man.[12]

Theistic phraseology and thought reappeared in the *Origin* itself. There, in the first edition, Darwin again referred to "the works of the Creator"[13] and concluded that "there is grandeur in this view of life, with its several powers, having been originally breathed into a few forms or into one; and that . . . from so simple a beginning endless forms most beautiful and most wonderful have been, and are being, evolved."[14] The two epigraphs on the frontispiece to the *Origin* likewise mentioned God and the Divine (terms Darwin himself usually avoided): the first quoted William Whewell's argument for thinking of nature in terms of general laws rather than "insulated interpositions of Di-

---

[8]Charles Darwin, "Essay" (1844), in *Evolution by Natural Selection*, ed. Gavin de Beer (Cambridge: Cambridge University Press, 1958) 114.

[9]Charles Darwin, *Charles Darwin's Natural Selection*, ed. R. C. Stauffer (Cambridge: Cambridge University Press, 1975) 353; cf. idem, *The Origin of Species, by Charles Darwin: A Variorum Text*, ed. Morse Peckham (Philadelphia: University of Pennsylvania Press, 1959) 343.

[10]Darwin, *Charles Darwin's Natural Selection*, ed. R. C. Stauffer, 224, 248.

[11]Ibid.

[12]*Autobiography*, 92-93.

[13]Peckham, *Variorum Text*, 344.

[14]Ibid., 759.

vine power''; the second quoted Francis Bacon's denial that ''a man can search too far or be too well studied in the book of God's word, or in the book of God's works.''[15]

While the presence of theistic language in the *Origin* is undeniable, its function is debatable. On the one hand, it is surely there partly because Darwin himself was still inclined to believe that nature's laws were originally designed and created by a higher, intelligent power. Indeed, in 1878, when the Reverend Dr. Pusey labeled the *Origin* an attack on religion, Darwin retorted in hyperbolic fashion: ''When I was collecting facts for the 'Origin,' my belief in what is called a personal God was as firm as that of Dr. Pusey himself.''[16] On the other hand, Darwin also must have felt it was politic to show that on one basic point, at least, he was not at odds with a scientific or general public that, even when as liberal and unorthodox as Charles Lyell, was for the most part strongly theistic.[17] Darwin's extraordinary delay in offering his theories for public inspection was undoubtedly due in part to a concern for their reception by just such people.

Nevertheless, in keeping with his commitment to moving beyond the theological stage of science, Darwin wanted to avoid theological explanations of natural events that had occurred since the world's creation. To that end, he mostly refrained from using traditional religious terminology. In the first edition of the *Origin* he used the word ''God'' only once in the body of the text, and that was in refuting an assumption of the special creationists.[18] When needing to refer specifically to God, Darwin preferred the term ''Creator,'' which could be interpreted purely functionally, although it also carried ''Pentateuchal'' connotations he later regretted. Never did he himself use such terms as ''the Lord,'' ''the Almighty,'' ''Providence,'' or even (except in quotations) ''Deity'' or ''Divine.'' In his science, it seems, he was prepared only to treat the Designer as a hypothetical intelligent First Cause, not as an omnipotent and omniscient supernatural agent nor as an object of worship.[19]

When the *Origin* first appeared, it met with such criticism from certain members of the religious and scientific establishments that Darwin felt a mixture of shock and consternation. Seldom one to enjoy polemic, Darwin tried to fend off future criticism by amending the text of the second edition, which appeared less than two months after the first. To the previous epigraphs he added another, this one from Joseph Butler's famous work of natural theology, the *Analogy of Religion* (1736), which stated that what is natural ''as

---

[15]Ibid., ii.

[16]*LLD*, 2:412.

[17]For Darwin's expressed admiration for Lyell's religious liberalism, see *Autobiography*, 100.

[18]See Paul H. Barrett, Donald J. Weinshank, and Timothy T. Gottleber, eds., *A Concordance to Darwin's Origin of Species, First Edition* (Ithaca NY: Cornell University Press, 1981).

[19]See, e.g., *LLD*, 2:6-7, 45.

much requires and presupposes an intelligent agent to render it so, i.e. to effect it continually or at stated times, as what is supernatural or miraculous does to effect it for once.''[20] Darwin's use of this quotation must have been intentionally ambiguous; certainly it was potentially deceptive, since he could hardly have supported the suggestion that the natural order requires either continuous or repeated action of ''an intelligent agent.'' Later in the book Darwin inserted a rather disingenuous avowal that he saw ''no good reason why the views given in this volume should shock the religious feelings of any one,'' and he took the opportunity to quote a letter from ''a celebrated divine'' testifying that its author (Charles Kingsley) had come to see that creation by means of a few original forms capable of self-development allowed ''just as noble a conception of the Deity'' as did a kind of creation that needed further special creative acts.[21] In addition, Darwin now twice went out of his way to specify the Creator as the original source of the breath of life.[22] One of these changes occurred in the climactic final paragraph. All in all, Darwin came far closer to conventional religious terminology than he had earlier and he ran the risk of seeming to resurrect a theological science that would see God as actively guiding the ongoing processes of nature.

It is understandable, then, that in 1863 Darwin could write to J. D. Hooker: ''I have long regretted that I truckled to public opinion, and used the Pentateuchal term of creation, by which I really meant 'appeared' by some wholly unknown process. It is mere rubbish, thinking at present of the origin of life; one might as well think of the origin of matter.''[23] These are strong words; but we should not surmise, as many have, that Darwin was denying he had any sympathy whatsoever with theism. In that case his various reminiscences to the contrary would have to be discounted, and the numerous instances of theistic language in previous essays and preliminary drafts would have to be seen as prevarications feebly trying to placate imagined critics. It is more plausible to suppose Darwin's concern in his letter to Hooker was rather that talk about the Creator's breath as the source of life had implicated God in an act of special creation subsequent to the original creation of matter, which to him was indeed a notion that was ''rubbish.'' In regretting such talk, Darwin was not necessarily wanting to rule God out altogether.[24] Instead, he was

---

[20]Peckham, *Variorum Text,* ii.

[21]Ibid., 748. Kingsley, a Broad Churchman whose orthodoxy was marginal, soon saw that acceptance of Darwin's theories would mean that ''all natural theology must be rewritten.'' See Mandelbaum, ''Darwin's Religious Views,'' *J. Hist. Ideas* 19 (1958): 308n.

[22]Peckham, *Variorum Text,* 753, 759.

[23]*LLD,* 2:202-203.

[24]That the wish to avoid special creationist language lies behind Darwin's comments to Hooker is corroborated by Darwin's response to Lyell's criticisms after the latter had received an advance copy of the *Origin:* ''We must under present knowledge assume the creation of one or a few forms in the same manner as philosophers assume the existence of a power of attraction without any explanation. But I entirely reject, as in my judgment quite unnecessary, any sub-

wishing he had been courageous enough to be consistently naturalistic and materialistic in his explanations of events within natural history.

Not that Darwin is likely to have decided that he should have flaunted his naturalistic and materialist views. Two decades before the *Origin*, he had reminded himself in the "M" notebook (1838) of the need to avoid stating how far he believed in "materialism."[25] But in the still earlier "C" notebook he had said, when recalling early astronomers like Galileo, that scientists must remember that "if they *believe* [disturbing ideas] & do not openly avow their belief they do as much to retard [as others have to advance] the truth."[26] Darwin liked to think that, in contrast to Galileo, he would not compromise his integrity by being less than perfectly honest. In an 1879 letter he averred, "I fully believe and hope that I have never written a word, which at the time I did not think."[27] His abhorrence of conflict, however, caused him at times to fall short of this ideal: witness, for example, his willingness in conversation to let Alfred Lord Tennyson continue to suppose that evolution "does not make against Christianity."[28] In any case, at the time he wrote Hooker, the question of scientific courage and honesty was definitely on his mind. Just a month before, Darwin had complained to Hooker that Lyell thought of himself as having all the "courage of a martyr of old," whereas he was really too timid to speak out on the evolution of species.[29] The remark about his own "truckling," then, surely reflects Darwin's irritation at having hastily compromised his science and having perhaps "retarded" the truth by conjuring an image of miraculous divine intervention. What it does not reflect is an abiding and hitherto disguised antipathy toward theism.

Be that as it may, by 1863 Darwin's theism would have disturbed any conventionally religious person; whatever its function, it did not undergird traditional affirmations concerning either divine or human nature. During the remainder of the 1860s and early 1870s it was at a low ebb indeed, often subsiding into agnosticism.

---

sequent addition 'of new powers and attributes and forces;' or of any 'principles of improvement'. . . . If I were convinced that I required additions to the theory of natural selection, I would reject it as rubbish," *LLD*, 2:6. One notes that here, if "new powers and attributes" were required, Darwin would regard his own theory as rubbish; in his letter to Hooker he declares that it is the implication that such new acts of divine power are required that is itself rubbish. Cf. his letter to T. H. Huxley, *LLD*, 2:45. See also Neal Gillespie's discussion of this issue, *Darwin and Creation* (Chicago: University of Chicago Press, 1979) 134-36.

[25]"M" notebook, 57.

[26]"Transmutation Notebook C," 123-24.

[27]*LLD*, 1:275.

[28]Quoted in Gillespie, *Darwin and Creation*, 143.

[29]*LLD*, 2:194.

CHAPTER 4

A MUDDLE

For the rest of Darwin's life his beliefs concerning the possible existence of some sort of God never entirely ceased to ebb and flow, nor did his evaluation of the merit of such beliefs. At low tide, so to speak, he was essentially an undogmatic atheist; at high tide he was a tentative theist; the rest of the time he was basically agnostic—in sympathy with theism but unable or unwilling to commit himself on such imponderable questions. Overall his thoughts regarding theological matters could best be described as being in what he himself termed a "muddle."

With a few exceptions, previously noted, scholars who have believed Darwin was a theist up until the publication of the *Origin* have held that he was clearly an agnostic from the early 1860s until his death in 1882. (The rumored death-bed "conversion" is not supported by a shred of evidence.)[1] When applied to the last decade of Darwin's life, moreover, the term "agnostic" has been used as the equivalent of "undogmatic atheist."[2] This view, like the one that sees Darwin as an agnostic or perhaps even an atheist from 1840 on, misses the complexity and perplexity of Darwin's attitudes. It is true that his theism, severely shaken in the late 1830s, was barely fit to survive the inner and outer controversies that surrounded the publication of the *Origin*. Yet in the early 1860s, when Darwin confessed himself bewildered and in a theological "muddle," he also professed to be unable, nonetheless, to keep away from questions of design and providence posed not only by himself but also by Asa Gray, Charles Lyell, and others.[3] As late as 1870 he wrote to Hooker:

---

[1]The legend of Darwin's deathbed conversion seems to have been fabricated by one Lady Hope, an evangelist whose claim to have been present at Darwin's death is contradicted by the testimony of others who were undeniably present, including Darwin's daughter Henrietta. See Ronald W. Clark, *The Survival of Charles Darwin: A Biography of a Man and an Idea* (New York: Random House, 1984) 199.

[2]Maurice Mandelbaum, "Darwin's Religious Views," *J. Hist. Ideas* 19 (1958): 376, 378.

[3]*LLD*, 1:283; *LLD*, 2:104-106, 174-75.

"Your conclusion that all speculation about preordination is idle waste of time is the only wise one; but how difficult it is not to speculate! My theology is a simple muddle; I cannot look at the universe as the result of blind chance, yet I see no evidence of beneficent design, or indeed of design of any kind, in the details."[4]

This is not to deny that Darwin often wearied of theological discussion and that much of what he did say from the 1860s on was unmistakably agnostic, and sometimes atheistic, in tenor. In Darwin's famous conversation in 1881 with the militant Marxists Edward Aveling and Ludwig Büchner, he seems to have assented to Aveling's suggestion that his position was little more than a nonaggressive version of their atheism.[5] Darwin's son Francis, present at the time, later criticized Aveling's account of the conversation and tried to differentiate his father's outlook from Aveling's. But he did not ascribe to his father's statements a more positive religious content, only a less dogmatic and assertive tone.[6] Previously, in a letter Darwin wrote to Aveling in 1880, he noted that "direct arguments against Christianity and Theism hardly have any effect on the public" and expressed a preference for gradual enlightenment through science.[7] A similar attitude was conveyed in his responses to his son George's attacks on religion, with the difference that theistic belief per se escaped criticism.[8] While eschewing ardent atheism, Darwin was hardly embracing ardent theism.

It should again be remembered, however, that Darwin would not have wanted simply to equate criticism of religion with criticism of theism; from Paley he would have learned that the theist, instead of relying on special revelation, might look to a strictly natural theology for evidence. For Paley himself, to be sure, natural theology was intended not to supplant "revealed" theology and religion but to supplement it, facilitating belief in the "fundamental articles of *Revelation*" such as the resurrection of the dead or the divinity of Christ.[9] Paley argued, however, that even for one who cannot accept revelation, theism is rationally credible and in fact more credible than the alternatives. It is consistent, therefore, that Darwin's attitude toward religion as such could differ greatly from his attitude toward belief in God.

---

[4]*MLD*, 1:321.

[5]See Edward Aveling, *The Religious Views of Charles Darwin* (London: Freethought, 1883). Aveling, who was the common law son-in-law of Karl Marx, cannot be assumed to be a disinterested listener or reporter.

[6]*LLD*, 1:286.

[7]Quoted in Howard E. Gruber, *Darwin on Man: A Psychological Study of Scientific Creativity*, 2d ed. (Chicago: University of Chicago Press, 1981) 27. Until recently it was thought that the letter was written to Karl Marx.

[8]See Peter Brent, *Charles Darwin: "A Man of Enlarged Curiosity"* (New York: Harper & Row, 1981) 453-54.

[9]Paley, *Natural Theology*, chap. 27 (Paley's capitalization and italics).

In truth, close scrutiny of the evidence reveals that, despite Darwin's re-jection of Christianity and religion, he never adopted a stance that was totally unsympathetic toward theism, let alone staunchly atheistic. Ironically, Aveling's own pamphlet gives clues supporting this very point, although Aveling has often been interpreted as providing strong evidence that Darwin eventually settled into an agnosticism that was atheistic in all but name. As Aveling admits, Darwin expressed sympathy with his guests' atheism only when Aveling and Büchner explained that the "true" sort of atheism that they espoused did not entail the "folly" of "God-denial." Rather, it was merely the refusal to commit the equal "folly" of positively affirming God's exis-tence and of placing one's hope in a supernatural world. It was strictly this closely circumscribed kind of atheism that Darwin acknowledged to be sim-ilar to his own outlook, which he still preferred to call "agnostic."

What is more, Aveling's record of the ensuing conversation gives hints of a degree of ambivalence even within Darwin's avowed agnosticism. Aveling writes that he respectfully questioned Darwin about his having included in the *Origin of Species* the well-known passages alluding to the Creator's breath as the source of primordial life. Apparently Darwin did not reiterate the regrets that, unknown to Aveling, he had long before expressed to Hooker. Indeed, after Aveling ventured to ask Darwin whether it was not unscientific and in-consistent to have invoked supernatural intervention as something "essential to the origin of life," Darwin made no reply but became, in Aveling's words, "silent and thoughtful for a space." Later in the conversation, Aveling was pleased to hear Darwin lament that so much energy is "wasted" on religion and on theological speculation when it could be used for the betterment of life on earth. Yet it is obvious from the way Aveling concludes his pamphlet that he had left Darwin's residence with the impression that a distance remained between Darwin's theological views and his own. Although he hails his late "Master" as a kind of secular prophet of the new age and jubilantly reports how Darwin had cast off the "old bonds" of Christianity, Aveling comments that Darwin himself may never have fully recognized the negative theological consequences of his theories.[10]

We have other, much less ambiguous evidence that Darwin continued all his life to think that theism warranted more serious intellectual consideration than did any historical religion. It is noteworthy, for example, that Darwin's autobiographical account of his struggles with theism differs markedly from his account of his rejection of revealed religion. The *Autobiography* recalls that, considerably after Darwin's rejection of Christianity, theism itself be-gan to seem to him difficult to justify. It argues that the law of natural selec-

---

[10]Aveling, *Religious Views of Darwin,* 5-8. Aveling may have confused matters both in his conversation with Darwin and in his report of it, by continually referring to belief in God as belief in the "supernatural." Darwin himself seldom, if ever, used such terminology. At any rate, Aveling's account has been so often misrepresented that one is forced to wonder whether it has not been more frequently cited than read.

tion made Paley obsolete, because now one had no need of the idea of God or providential design to explain the beautifully effective hinge of a bivalve shell or even more perfect adaptations. The *Autobiography* questions, too, whether the existence of a good, omniscient, and omnipotent God could be compatible with the amount of suffering in the world; whether belief in any sort of intelligent and just God is as universal as has been supposed; and whether such feelings as give rise to belief in God are trustworthy in any event. Although Darwin notes that he once had such feelings himself, especially in natural surroundings, he now regards them as varieties of the sense of the sublime and hence as subjective and of dubious evidential value. Belief in the immortality of the soul, being linked to just such feelings, must likewise be suspect.

Yet the *Autobiography* pinpoints another source for conviction in the existence of God—the most important one, Darwin says, and one not connected with feelings so much as with reason. What is most persuasive, he claims, is "the extreme difficulty *or rather impossibility* of conceiving this immense and wonderful universe, including man, . . . as the result of blind chance or necessity." When thus reflecting, Darwin admits, "I feel compelled to look to a First Cause having an intelligent mind in some degree analogous to that of man; and I deserve to be called a Theist."[11] The present tense of this statement shows it is not to be understood as mere reminiscence. But Darwin acknowledges that his theistic belief has, since his writing of the *Origin of Species,* "very gradually with many fluctuations become weaker." It has particularly been undermined by the doubt that a mind that has evolved from the "lowest animal" is to be trusted when it tries to draw "such grand conclusions."[12] That belief in God persists in some form even in himself could mean merely that it is instinctive, like a monkey's fear of snakes; sheer persistence is no guarantee that the belief is warranted. For this reason, Darwin writes, "I for one must be content to remain an Agnostic" (a term he borrows from Huxley).[13] Although this sounds final, Darwin immediately goes on to characterize himself, and by implication any other "agnostic," as a person "who has no *assured and ever present belief* in the existence of a personal God or of a future existence with retribution and reward"—a person, therefore, whose rule for life must be to follow the morality dictated by the best "impulses and instincts."[14] By this description, an agnostic might some-

---

[11]*Autobiography,* 85-93; quotation from 92-93 (emphasis added).

[12]Ibid., 93.

[13]Mandelbaum ("Darwin's Religious Views," *J. Hist. Ideas* 19 [1958]: 373n) discusses the derivation of the term from Huxley. It will be evident that I disagree with his interpretation of what Darwin himself meant by the term. For Huxley, at any rate, agnosticism meant nothing less than the death of any sort of theology. See Thomas H. Huxley, "Agnosticism," in his *Science and Christian Tradition: Essays* (1897; reprint ed., New York: Greenwood Press, 1968) 250.

[14]*Autobiography,* 94 (emphasis added).

times believe in God: the belief simply would not be "assured and ever present." This is a far cry from "nonaggressive atheism."

Significantly, in all this discussion Darwin never once says he is or has been *neutral* in his attitude toward the possibility of God's existence. Nor does he say what he said about his former belief in Christianity and revelation—that it is completely gone, and for the good. On the contrary, he insists that it is still sometimes impossible for him to conceive of the overall design of the universe as having come about by chance. He calls himself an agnostic, but his agnosticism is then described as tantamount only to an abiding uncertainty as to whether his intermittent sense that the world's design requires a Designer is truly rational and trustworthy. In short, Darwin's agnosticism does not entirely eradicate his theistic belief, which seems to him almost innate; it questions whether the belief is backed by appropriate evidence.

Darwin's correspondence likewise gives us every reason to think that the tensions between theism and agnosticism, or between varying degrees of agnosticism, stayed with him from the years immediately following the *Origin* until his death in 1882. In 1879, during the time in which the *Autobiography* was written, Darwin wrote in answer to J. Fordyce's questions about his religious beliefs: "My judgment *often fluctuates*. . . . In my most extreme fluctuations I have never been an Atheist in the sense of denying the existence of God. I think that generally (and more and more as I grow older), *but not always,* that an Agnostic would be the more correct description of my state of mind."[15] In 1873 he wrote to a Dutch student: "I may say that the *impossibility of conceiving that this grand and wondrous universe,* with our conscious selves, arose through chance, seems to me the chief argument for the existence of God; but whether this is an argument of real value, I *have never been able to decide.*"[16] To Julia Wedgwood, Darwin had written in 1861: "The mind *refuses* to look at this universe, being what it is, without having been designed; yet, where one would most expect design, viz. in the structure of a sentient being, the more I think on the subject, the less I can see proof of design."[17] In correspondence with Asa Gray he said something similar: "I am in an utterly hopeless muddle. I cannot think that the world, as we see it, is the result of chance; and yet I cannot look at each separate thing as the re-

---

[15]*LLD,* 1:274 (emphasis added). In the same context (although in words not found in this edition of the letters) Darwin opined: "What my own views may be is a question of no consequence to anyone except myself"—an opinion shared by virtually no one else. He nevertheless made the observation that it seemed to him "absurd to doubt that a man may be an ardent theist & an evolutionist. . . . Whether a man deserves to be called a theist depends on the definition of the term, which is much too large a subject for a note." Quoted in A. Hunter Dupree, "Christianity and the Scientific Community in the Age of Darwin," in *God and Nature: Historical Essays on the Encounter Between Christianity and Science,* ed. David C. Lindberg and Ronald L. Numbers (Berkeley: University of California Press, 1986) 365.

[16]Ibid., 276 (emphasis added).

[17]Ibid., 283 (emphasis added).

sult of Design.''[18] These words are almost duplicated in the 1870 letter to Hooker quoted above.[19] In a letter to William Graham, author of *The Creed of Science* (1881), Darwin said that, although he could not agree with Graham's contention that the existence of ''so-called natural laws'' implies purpose, Graham's book had nonetheless captured his interest more than any other he had read in a very long time: ''You have expressed *my inward conviction,* though far more vividly and clearly than I could have done, that *the Universe is not the result of chance.* But then with me the *horrid doubt* always arises whether the convictions of man's mind, which has been developed from the mind of the lower animals, are of any value or at all trustworthy.''[20]

Finally, there is the Duke of Argyll's record of a conversation held with Darwin in 1882, the last year of his life. After the Duke remarked that he could not ponder the purposeful contrivances of nature described in Darwin's works without ''seeing they were the effect and the expression of mind,'' Darwin reportedly looked at him ''very hard and said, 'Well, that *often* comes over me *with overwhelming force;* but at other times,' and he shook his head vaguely, adding, 'it seems to go away.' ''[21]

The picture that emerges is remarkably clear, for all the ambivalence it reveals on Darwin's part. As the italicized phrases in the above quotations show, Darwin in his later years took a skeptical attitude toward his theistic thoughts and feelings; yet they recurred intermittently until his death. In view of the ambiguity of the evidence and the limitations of the mind, his agnosticism, verging sometimes on theism and sometimes on atheism, was itself uncertain. Furthermore, Darwin's doubts about God, unlike his earlier doubts about Christianity, did not strike him on the whole as liberating. He characterized them with negative adjectives such as ''horrid''; he said the theological questions raised by his work were ''always painful'' to him, avowing that he wished he could see clearer evidence of design and beneficence in the world.[22] The concomitant doubts about immortality led him, moreover, to what he termed ''an intolerable thought''—that human beings, who in the distant future will be ''far more perfect'' creatures than now, are eventually doomed to complete annihilation, individually and as a species.[23]

There is thus good reason to disagree with Darwin's recent and best biographer, Peter Brent, when he concludes that Darwin was simply apathetic toward the question of overarching purpose and hence of God, that he contentedly made science his god instead, and that for political and domestic reasons he dressed up his purely vestigial religious feelings in the guise of

---

[18]*LLD*, 2:146.

[19]*MLD*, 1:321.

[20]*LLD*, 1:284-85 (emphasis added); cf. *MLD*, 1:395.

[21]*LLD*, 1:285 (emphasis added).

[22]*LLD*, 2:105.

[23]*Autobiography*, 92.

''earnest agnosticism.''[24] We have seen that this interpretation of the data is simply not plausible if one chooses to believe Darwin himself—which means believing that a human being can vacillate, experiencing ineradicable intellectual tensions and recurrent ambivalence. This being the case, what remains to be found is a more complete explanation of the factors involved in Darwin's ambivalence when reflecting on God and the world's design. We will then have a better understanding of why Darwin's theism, after ceasing to evolve, neither flourished nor completely died out.

---

[24]Brent, *Charles Darwin,* 456-57. A still more recent biography, Clark's *The Survival of Charles Darwin,* says little about Darwin's theological and religious reflections, thereby giving the impression that the author is of much the same opinion as Brent.

CHAPTER 5

AN ELUSIVE GOD,
AN ANXIOUS SELF,
AND A PERPLEXING WORLD

It is well known that shortly after their marriage, and again two years after the publication of the *Origin of Species,* Emma Darwin wrote Charles regarding his religious beliefs. Both of her letters expressed concern. While reflecting no technical knowledge either of science or of theology, they were by no means naive. The first letter tactfully and lovingly voiced fears that Darwin's habitually scientific way of thinking, along with the anti-religious influence of his brother Erasmus, had made him mistrust truths that lie beyond the bounds of science and had cut him off from a proper sense of reverence before the revelations of God's grace. Emma agreed with Charles's conviction that matters of moral duty were unaffected by his theories—a point on which he always insisted—but felt that his thinking would rule out acts of piety, such as prayer, and implied that it left in doubt the prospect of immortality. ''I should be most unhappy if I thought we did not belong to each other for ever,'' she wrote. The letter closed with a declaration of love and with wishes for Charles's happiness. Moved to the point of tears, Charles wrote at the end: ''When I am dead, know that many times, I have kissed and cryed over this. C. D.'' The second letter was written at a time during which Charles was suffering acutely from the illness that persisted for much of his life. Like the first letter, this one urged him to consider the limits of reason, the value of prayer, the care of God in times of suffering. It, too, was tender and deeply appreciative, prompting Charles to respond: ''God bless you.''[1]

It has been common to think of Emma Darwin in somewhat negative or condescending terms, claiming she inhibited Charles's expression not only

---

[1]''Mrs. Darwin's Papers on Religion,'' *Autobiography,* 235-38.

of his views on religion but also of those scientific views that might disturb orthodox believers. This accusation is not totally without justification. Of the nearly six thousand words expurgated from the first edition of the *Autobiography* (published posthumously), many that were critical of religion were omitted at her request. It is also noteworthy that, regarding the *Descent of Man* (1871), parts of which Emma read prior to publication, she remarked: "I think it will be very interesting, but that I shall dislike it very much as again putting God further off."[2] Charles himself wrote, late in life, "Possibly I have been too strongly influenced by the thought of the concern it might cause some members of my family, if in any way I lent my support to direct attacks on religion."[3] Considerations such as these are what have prompted scholars like Brent to believe that Darwin's continued expression of a degree of openness to theistic ideas and speculations was externally motivated, a disguise for what amounted to a benign, tranquil, and truly disinterested atheism.

What is easily overlooked is that Emma Darwin was not particularly orthodox in religious views and that her belief in Christianity was not uncritical. She taught her children a Unitarian creed;[4] she opposed the doctrine of everlasting punishment as inconsistent with genuine Christianity; and she evidently would not commit herself to the idea of the verbal inspiration of Scripture.[5] According to her daughter Henrietta, "She kept a sorrowful wish to believe more, and . . . it was an abiding sadness to her that her faith was less vivid than it had been in her youth."[6] Emma was thus not ill equipped to consider Charles's questions, although they would worry her. In any case, Charles disregarded his father's advice to conceal from her all his doubts, and there is good reason to think he allowed her to learn of his evolutionary theories well before the publication of the *Origin*.[7] Her two letters to Charles, although (as she says) not written with any strong expectation of persuading him, certainly touched on key issues: the nature of scientific and religious

---

[2]Henrietta Litchfield, ed., *Emma Darwin: A Century of Family Letters, 1796-1896*, 2 vols. (New York: D. Appleton, 1915) 2:196.

[3]Quoted in Howard E. Gruber, *Darwin on Man: A Psychological Study of Scientific Creativity*, 2d ed. (Chicago: University of Chicago Press, 1981) 27n.

[4]"Mrs. Darwin's Papers," *Autobiography*, 238.

[5]Ibid., 87n.

[6]Litchfield, *Emma Darwin*, 2:173. Emma Darwin's letters corroborate Henrietta Litchfield's judgment that her mother's religious feelings became less vivid and her beliefs less orthodox as years went by. Emma's correspondence also shows her to have had, all along, a lively and independent mind. In their letters she and Charles both occasionally make fun of self-righteous piety and legalism. Like Charles, she cannot abide the vengeful tone of the Psalms, and she is scornful of religious intolerance and of forms of Christianity that dwell on sin and guilt. Moreover, she refuses to pass judgment on the contemporary "race of agnostics," while expressing some sadness that "age disperses [religious] feelings, especially with thoughtful men." See *Emma Darwin*, 2:53, 173-75, 196, 201, 285, 302-306.

[7]See Gruber, *Darwin on Man*, 27.

evidence, the limits of human life and understanding, the problem of suffering, and God's relation to the world. In his own way, Charles pondered these very matters on his own and, as we have seen, would sometimes confess himself in a "muddle" as to what to make of them. It is possible that he sometimes continued to find himself a theist of sorts—what one is tempted to term an "agnostic theist"—precisely because he could not entirely dismiss feelings, thoughts, and concerns that in part he shared in common with Emma, even if he could never agree with her about revelation or prayer or Christian faith.

One thing is certain: Charles's air of sagacious serenity, which made him seem far removed from such concerns as those Emma expressed, was belied by certain letters, notebooks, and other evidence not available to the public during his lifetime and only partially taken into account even now. Indications of considerable inner turmoil are found throughout the early notebooks, often in introspective observations that flatly contradict Charles's much later claim that he had never tried looking into his own mind.[8] In the "M" and "N" notebooks, for instance, a disproportionate amount of the discussion of emotions is given to analyzing anger and other hostile or negative feelings. Many of these feelings are described on the basis of personal experience. He recalls, for example, "an insane feeling of anger" that came over him one evening when he was tired and idly listening to music. Elsewhere he notes that he had actually tried skipping when "wanting not to feel angry."[9] Whereas the autobiographical dimension is naturally minimized in his later volume *The Expression of the Emotions in Man and Animals* (1872), anger, fear, shame, disgust, defiance, and various other signs or feelings of hostility receive a conspicuous amount of attention there as well. Francis Darwin tells us, moreover, that when his ordinarily quiet and gentle father felt strongly about a question, "he could hardly trust himself to speak, as he then easily became angry, a thing which he disliked excessively."[10]

It seems probable that Darwin's expressions of anger, his intense concern for hostile feelings, and the ease with which he was disturbed by the outside world were symptomatic of a mind characterized by inner conflict and anxiety. It is also likely that inner tensions played a part in his mysterious, debilitating illness—a forty-year sickness that included periodically severe eczema, headaches, and dizziness as well as nausea and vomiting that plagued him almost daily for months at a time, keeping him in virtual seclusion for most of his maturity and restricting his workday to a few hours.[11] When one considers that this illness was in large part gastrointestinal, that no one tried

---

[8]*LLD*, 2:414.

[9]"M" notebook, 51, 70.

[10]*LLD*, 1:118.

[11]For a thorough and fascinating study of Darwin's illness, see Ralph Colp, *To Be an Invalid: The Illness of Charles Darwin* (Chicago: University of Chicago Press, 1977).

to deny it was drastically affected by anxieties, and that Darwin himself understood the stomach to be an organ within which, as he said, "lie intellect, conscience, temper & the affections," so that the stomach's disturbance was in his view a moral and physical evil[12]—considering all this, one realizes that Darwin was not blessed with inner serenity. Thus, if he left certain crucial theological issues unresolved and eventually kept them at an emotional and intellectual distance, he did not necessarily do so because of apathy; in point of fact, it was probably because he found himself unable to contemplate such large issues with equanimity. Darwin, at any rate, explicitly asserted that his health, which he himself understood to be related to his mental state, had been a factor in his not undertaking systematic reflection on religious and moral questions and their connection with science.[13]

On one theological matter more than any other Darwin's sensitivity, indeed hypersensitivity, seems to have had considerable bearing: the question of the place of suffering in the world's design, and the connection of God with a world of such suffering. Examining Darwin's response to this question, we see the clearest indication of why Darwin's ambivalent "agnostic theism" could not resolve itself into either atheism or confident belief.

Of all the people to reflect on natural evil and its theological implications, Darwin was among those most acutely aware of, and repelled by, creaturely suffering. His sensitivity to suffering was in fact described by Francis Darwin as "one of the strongest feelings in his nature."[14] When fishing, he took care not to put live worms on the hook, but first killed them mercifully in a brine solution.[15] He eventually gave up the hunting he loved so much, feeling guilty for having derived pleasure from cruelty.[16] Opposed to the indiscriminate practice of vivisection, Darwin spoke of the "infinite sufferings of animals—not only those [sufferings] of the body, but those of the mind," and seriously attributed to all sorts of animals many of the emotions and much of the mentality associated with human beings.[17] Naturally he could not stand to see animals mistreated—or humans made into slaves and treated as badly as the other animals.[18] In the early "B" notebook he said that if we "let conjecture run wild" (and in this case that was his inclination), then we will regard animals "our fellow brethren in pain, disease death & suffering & famine, our slaves in most laborious work, our companion in our amusements. . . . [From] our

---

[12]*MLD*, 1:78-79.

[13]*LLD*, 1:276-77.

[14]*LLD*, 2:377.

[15]*Autobiography*, 27; cf. 45 and his early reluctance to kill insects for his collection.

[16]*LLD*, 1:142; cf. *Autobiography*, 55.

[17]*MLD*, 1:395; *LLD*, 2:377-87; *LLD*, 1:95; Charles Darwin, *The Expression of the Emotions in Man and Animals (1872)* (New York: D. Appleton, 1899) passim.

[18]*LLD*, 2:377-78, 166.

origin in one common ancestor we may be all netted together.''[19] Darwin's affection extended to plant life. Toward a flower he would show, according to Francis, ''a kind of gratitude, and a personal love for its delicate form and color.''[20] Unnerved by other people's pain and by the sight of blood, Darwin was haunted for years after his brief medical training by the memory of two ''very bad operations'' he had witnessed.[21] As might be expected, in raising his children he avoided physical punishment.[22] The deaths of friends and relations shook him greatly. After his daughter Annie died at age ten, Darwin wrote a private, deeply felt eulogy for her and then could not bear to speak again of her death or to visit her grave.[23] He professed to be (and perhaps was) too ill to attend his own father's funeral and would not visit his dying former mentor Henslow, for fear of ''mental excitement'' that might upset his health.[24]

Obviously such a person would be profoundly disturbed by the world envisioned by the theory of natural selection. Very early on, Darwin wrote in one of his notebooks, ''It is difficult to believe in the dreadful but quiet war of organic beings, going [on] in peaceful woods, & smiling fields.''[25] He was in fact all too aware of this ''war of nature,''[26] of its ''incalculable waste,'' and of the ''delight'' some animals seem to take in cruelty.[27] Given the harshness of the story told by natural history, it is little wonder that the novels he forever wanted Emma to read to him all needed to have happy endings and to feature some ''person one can thoroughly love.''[28]

Whatever one might say of the alleged Designer of the world that Darwin observed, this was not the sort of being he could ''thoroughly love.'' Paley might have been able sincerely to say, ''It is a happy world after all. The air, the earth, the water, teem with delighted existence. . . . [The fry of fish] are so happy, that they know not what to do with themselves. Their attitudes, . . . their frolics, . . . all conduce to show their excess of spirits.''[29] For Dar-

---

[19]''Transmutation Notebook B,'' 232.

[20]*LLD*, 1:94-95.

[21]Ibid., 113; *Autobiography*, 48.

[22]See Charles Darwin, ''A Biographical Sketch of an Infant,'' in Barrett and Gruber, 212.

[23]See Colp, *To Be an Invalid*, 75; and Litchfield, *Emma Darwin*, 2:137-39. Darwin does mention Annie's death in the *Autobiography*, 98.

[24]See Colp, *To Be an Invalid*, 39, 70-71.

[25]''Transmutation Notebook E,'' 114.

[26]Morse Peckham ed., *The Origin of the Species, by Charles Darwin: A Variorum Text*, (Philadelphia: University of Pennsylvania Press, 1959) 759.

[27]*The Foundations of the Origin of Species*, 51-52.

[28]*Autobiography*, 138-39.

[29]William Paley, *Natural Theology Selections*, (Indianalpolis: Bobbs-Merrill, 1963) chap. 26.

win the natural scene was, by contrast, that of competition and struggle. Paley could cheerfully declare that "few diseases are fatal" and proceed to support his claim with a hospital record summarizing six years of patients:[30]

Admitted 6420
Cured 5476
Dead 234

Darwin, more than anyone, would have been aware that they are *all* dead now and that the species itself is finally doomed.

Yet there is one statement of Paley's that Darwin could surely have endorsed: his assertion that "I have met with no serious person who thinks that, even under the Christian revelation, we have too much light."[31] In truth, Darwin thought the amount of light we have is far less than Paley imagined. By that limited light the world appeared to him at once designed and destructive, wonderful and terrible. It was this combination of the world's beautiful design with the horrible suffering of its creatures that, more than anything else, prevented Darwin from finding any satisfactory solution to his conflicting views concerning the credibility of theism.

In this connection, a crucial passage from Darwin's *Variation of Animals and Plants under Domestication* (1867) is illuminating, being one he often cited—most decisively in the *Autobiography*.[32] In the passage under consideration, Darwin declared it to be unbelievable that all the myriad and apparently random events of nature culminating in the use of particular stones for a particular building were actually foreseen in minute detail by an omniscient Creator and were therefore foreordained to a specific architectural end. Similarly, he thought it unbelievable that all the particular variations leading up to the "formation of the most perfectly adapted animals in the world, man included, were intentionally and specially guided." For if they were, then the whole concept of "the laws of nature" would be superfluous. One might as well think of natural occurrences as, without exception, acts of God. Furthermore, if the guiding plan and power were indeed that of an omnipotent and omniscient Creator, as Asa Gray and others supposed, one would have to wonder at the harshness and indirection of means: so many "injurious deviations of structure" and such a fierce struggle on the part of the creatures involved.[33]

Taking up this last theme, the *Autobiography* introduces a variation. It maintains that most sentient beings experience an excess of happiness over misery, since this is useful for survival and hence for natural selection. Yet—lest Paley seem to be resurrected—Darwin argues that the quantity of suffer-

---

[30]Ibid.

[31]"Preparatory Considerations," in *Evidences of Christianity.*

[32]*Autobiography,* 88.

[33]Charles Darwin, *The Variation of Animals and Plants Under Domestication,* 2 vols. (New York: D. Appleton, 1896) 2:427-28.

ing in the world, often benefiting no one and far transcending the merely human sphere, makes a "strong" case against the existence of a perfectly intelligent and good first cause. He leads up to this conclusion by way of a most provocative comment: "A being so powerful and so full of knowledge as a God who could create the universe, is to our finite minds omnipotent and omniscient, and it revolts our understanding to suppose that his benevolence is not unbounded, for what advantage can there be in the sufferings of millions of the lower animals throughout almost endless time?"[34]

It is to be noted that in these key (and somewhat confusing) passages Darwin never contends that it is *logically impossible* for all things to have been foreseen and directed by God. Rather, he claims that if the world's design were that encompassing and detailed, there would be no truly natural laws for science to study and, equally important, no God good enough to warrant the praise and admiration of moral creatures.[35]

Why, then, did Darwin not simply and completely let go of the whole idea of God? Why did he vacillate? There are several likely reasons why he did not turn purely atheistic or happily agnostic in his thinking. Among the most important is that, once having gone so far as to conceive of God as a being removed from direct control over natural events, Darwin had not only made room for a relatively autonomous science but had also blunted the sharpness of the theodicy question. As he wrote in one letter, "It has always appeared to me more satisfactory to look at the immense amount of pain and suffering in this world as the inevitable result of the natural sequence of events, i.e. general laws, rather than from the direct intervention of God."[36] Elsewhere he noted that he found it more acceptable to think that God was the creator of laws governing natural phenomena than to believe God would directly cause a particular bolt of lightning to kill a particular person.[37] The only God conceivable to Darwin would thus be, at most, responsible only for the overall design of things; the details, and hence much of the suffering, would be left to chance.

This heterodox but nonetheless genuine theodicy was hardly an afterthought. In his "Sketch of 1842" Darwin had already suggested that the orthodox view of God's pervasive activity in the world is derogatory of the Creator, in that creation includes such things as "creeping parasites" and cruel creatures that lay their eggs in the bowels and flesh of other animals. Following his own theory, these things supposedly cease to surprise us (though we may deplore them) because, he said, they are but the results of the secondary

---

[34] *Autobiography*, 88-90; cf. *LLD*, 1:276, where he says belief in God is hindered, for him, by "the immense amount of suffering through the world."

[35] For further reflections on suffering and design see *LLD*, 2:105-106, 165-66; *LLD*, 1:283-84.

[36] *LLD*, 2:247.

[37] Ibid., 105.

laws of a distant Creator. Besides which, he noted, the overall result of these laws is still good; for, in Darwin's words, "from death, famine, rapine, and the concealed war of nature we can see that the highest good, which we can conceive, the creation of the higher animals has directly come."[38]

Considering that such a radically revised natural theology would not only make God seem less cruel but would also, and hardly incidentally, leave room for the independence of science from theology, one recognizes that Darwin had indeed succeeded in minimizing, from his point of view, certain major liabilities of orthodox theologies. He was still at a loss about how to reconcile God's presumed omniscience and omnipotence with the facts that science established concerning the created order. After all, any world whose natural "secondary laws" result in widespread, random suffering would appear to have derived from an original design that was flawed either in conception or execution or both.[39] Yet Darwin's vision of a remote and restrained deity was evidently sufficient to make the idea of God less troublesome to him.

There was, in addition, a more positive reason for Darwin's recurrent attraction to some form of theism. It is found in his often repeated assertion that it seems impossible for a world so marvelously ordered (however imperfect in details) to have been the result of perfectly blind chance, of perfectly purposeless "laws."[40]

No doubt this line of reasoning appealed to Darwin partly because, as he says in his *Autobiography,* it seemed to him the most rational mode of trying to justify theism.[41] Yet Darwin's fascination with the argument from the world's encompassing order and beautiful design also suggests that the appeal of this notion had to do with more than its rational plausibility. Considering Darwin's worries over the problem of natural evil, one is struck by the fact that an overarching order designed by a distant God could potentially ameliorate those "natural" and "chance" effects of suffering and tragedy that appear to mar the world's beauty and that threaten any sanguine outlook on life. Indirectly their cause, Darwin's kind of God could also indirectly be their cure—not, of course, through active intervention but, rather, simply from having had an orderly plan that would, all things considered, turn out for the good. In short, a scientist who cared as Darwin did for the world's creatures and their destiny might take comfort in the likelihood that the end result of the earth's history would not be chaotic or senseless.

At times, one must admit, Darwin sounded as though he were of the opinion that nature's ways are tolerable and even admirable apart from any divine plan or purpose, though the "quiet war" of the natural world would be a moral embarrassment to any God who directly and deliberately manipulated each

---

[38]*The Foundations of the Origin of Species,* 51-52.

[39]See *LLD,* 2:105-106; *Variation of Animals and Plants,* 2:427-28.

[40]See *MLD,* 1:321.

[41]*Autobiography,* 92.

of its details. In the *Origin,* for instance, Darwin wrote: "We may console ourselves with the full belief, that the war of nature is not incessant, that no fear is felt, that death is generally prompt, and that the vigorous, the healthy, and the happy survive and multiply."[42]

Yet such words of consolation sound less than convincing in themselves and turn out to be connected with a view of the world that is neither completely scientific nor agnostic, let alone atheistic. In point of fact, Darwin could sound sanguine about the workings of nature chiefly because he treasured a high hope that human beings, as the culmination of nature's history up to now, will have a "secure future of . . . inappreciable length" in which all "corporeal and mental endowments [will] tend to progress towards perfection."[43] This high hope, a belief and trust in the progressive thrust of evolution, was in turn closely—if covertly—linked to a sense of overarching design and to belief in a Designer. This connection was openly acknowledged in the earlier volume *Natural Selection,* where Darwin explicitly referred to nature as "the laws ordained by God to govern the Universe" and in this context said that through nature "the good will be preserved & the bad rigidly destroyed."[44] Nature's mode of selection he described there as "gradual, steady, unerring, deep-sighted."[45]

A similar hope in progress and purpose was later reiterated in his work even when Darwin had no wish to connect this hope with the necessity of divinely providential planning. In the conclusion of *The Descent of Man,* for example, Darwin spoke of humans as having risen to "the very summit of the organic scale," with "a still higher *destiny* in the distant future."[46] But long before this book was published, Darwin had begun to vacillate on the question of whether there is scientific warrant for believing that evolutionary progress is inevitable and secure, and so in any sense "destined." In every edition of the *Origin of Species* he asserted that natural selection does *not* entail any fixed or universal

---

[42]Peckham, *Variorum Text,* 162.

[43]Ibid., 758.

[44]*Charles Darwin's Natural Selection,* 224.

[45]Ibid., 225.

[46]*Descent of Man,* 619 (emphasis added). Dov Ospovat has argued that Darwin's theory of natural selection was not originally a theory of progressive development but of adaptation— at first of "perfect" adaptation and later of "relative adaptedness." Yet from the first, Ospovat shows, Darwin envisioned change as essentially good, and by 1837 he did plainly believe in progress. During the 1850s, moreover, Darwin employed the idea of divergence to elaborate a theory of how progressive development occurs in nature. Even if some details of Ospovat's account are open to question, he is surely correct in pointing out that Darwin's early belief in perfect adaptation and his later belief in progress were both related to religious views he shared in common with many other naturalists and intellectuals of his day. See *Development of Darwin's Theory: Natural History, Natural Theology, and Natural Selection, 1838-1859* (Cambridge: Cambridge University Press, 1981), 230-35. See also Maurice Mandelbaum, *History, Man, and Reason: A Study in Nineteenth-Century Thought* (Baltimore: Johns Hopkins Press, 1971) 85-86; and Moore, *Post-Darwinian Controversies,* 160.

or necessary law of progressive development, and he overtly rejected Lamarck's theory that there is an ''innate and inevitable tendency towards perfection.''[47] In *The Descent of Man,* too, he denied that progress is an invariable rule or that there is some innate tendency towards ''continued development in mind and body.''[48] Though recent scholarship has shown beyond any reasonable doubt that Darwin thought his science confirmed his conviction that evolution is *on the whole* progressing toward the higher and the better, it remains the case that, in James Moore's words, ''natural selection, aided by the inherited effects of environment and habit, was an explanation of progress which could not ensure its . . . future inevitability.''[49] Certainly the kind of purposive selection and secure progress that Darwin had earlier attributed to nature on the presumption of its divine origin had come to seem barely more justifiable in strictly scientific terms than theism itself. In sum, Darwin's treasured hope for an ever brighter future was partly founded on, and furthered by, assumptions that transcended purely scientific evidence.

The same can be said, moreover, of Darwin's whole conception of what ''progress'' means. While he had mixed feelings about using terms such as ''higher'' or ''lower,'' Darwin nevertheless typically said that the forms of life that had ''progressed'' further were ''more advanced,'' ''higher,'' or ''more perfect'' than others.[50] The problem is that he meant more by such terms than he could justify scientifically. When exercising scientific caution and precision, he defined ''more advanced,'' ''more perfect,'' and ''higher'' life forms as simply those with more differentiated and specialized organs making them better adapted and more fit to survive.[51] This definition was basically descriptive and neutral. But Darwin's use of these terms often had value-laden connotations, and unmistakably so. Employing his own version of the idea of the Great Chain of Being, he implied that ''higher,'' ''more advanced,'' and ''more perfect'' beings such as humans are ontologically and morally superior: not merely competitively more fit, more specialized, and better adapted, but also genuinely ''nobler,'' more ''benevolent'' (a trait Darwin especially admired), and ''exalted.''[52] Here, as in his ideas concern-

---

[47]Peckham, *Variorum Text,* 223, 523, 567. Cf. *LLD,* 2:6.

[48]*Descent of Man,* 140-41.

[49]Moore, *Post-Darwinian Controversies,* 159; see also 158, 160. Darwin's views on progress are complex and much debated, as are issues related to the language he used to describe ''advanced'' forms of life. For some of the best discussions, see Mandelbaum, *History, Man, and Reason,* 77-88; Robert M. Young, ''Darwin's Metaphor: Does Nature Select?,'' *Monist* 55 (1971): 442-503; John C. Greene, *Science, Ideology, and World View* (Berkeley: University of California Press, 1981) 95-157 passim; and Ospovat, *The Development of Darwin's Theory,* 210-35.

[50]See, for instance, Darwin's letters to Hooker, *LLD,* 1:498; *MLD,* 1:76, 114-15.

[51]See *Descent of Man,* 91, and Peckham, *Variorum Text,* 221-22.

[52]See *Descent of Man,* 618-19. Mandelbaum and others have pointed out the tension between the language strictly appropriate to naturalistic science and the value-laden discourse used by Darwin. Yet, as Mandelbaum notes, the fact that Darwin's language reflected as-

ing progress, Darwin's convictions went beyond the evidence and bounds of purely naturalistic science.

Hence it seems clear that when Darwin formed and expressed his ideas of progress in the fullest sense, he drew on nonscientific sources, including theology. In his later years, Darwin's latent and intermittent attraction to theism not only paralleled but also surely helped reinforce the positive hope for creation reflected in the progressive view of evolution he believed in for scientific and quasi-scientific reasons. This suggests that both his theism and his belief in progress reflected a lingering and often unacknowledged need that had once been satisfied, for him, by Paley: a need for the world to have a design (however general) and a Designer (however remote). Altogether, his theologically colored beliefs in design and progress must have lent a certain impetus, not to mention grandeur, to Darwin's science itself; for his work could then be seen as the autonomous discernment of natural laws whereby an awesome though largely inscrutable design was being realized.

Darwin's deep reservations about a science in any way connected with theology did not disappear, however; as we have seen, he increasingly distrusted his attraction toward even a minimal theism. Having professed his bewilderment, Darwin distanced himself further and further from the troubling and confusing questions of theology. At the same time, his sense of the world's beneficent design waned and, with passing years, so did his sense of the sublimity of nature (a phenomenon he himself likened to becoming color-blind).[53] There is unmistakable poignancy in Darwin's assertion late in life that he had become "a kind of machine for grinding general laws out of large collections of facts"; he himself regarded this "a loss of happiness" perhaps injurious to the intellect and more probably to the "moral character."[54] In 1868, when

---

sumptions that derived from theology and from the metaphysical concept of the great chain of being was not unusual for his time. Other nineteenth-century thinkers such as Spencer and Mill used hierarchical and progressive language without any express theological intent and without seeing its incompatibility with naturalistic (or positivist) science. Given his sympathies with theism, however, Darwin had even more "excuse" for employing such language. See Mandelbaum, *History, Man, and Reason*, 87-88; cf. Greene, *Science, Ideology, and World View*, 135-40; and Ospovat, *The Development of Darwin's Theory*, 227-28.

[53]*Autobiography*, 91. John Angus Campbell argues persuasively that Darwin's "affective decline" was not strictly correlated with his loss of religious faith and that his love of nature persisted to the end ("Nature, Religion, and Emotional Response: A Reconsideration of Darwin's Affective Decline," *Victorian Studies* 18 [1974]: 159-74). It is nevertheless true that Darwin described the intensity of his experience of nature as having been somehow altered and diminished by his increasing insensitivity to the aesthetic, the sublime, and the divine. It is this that he likened to having become color-blind and to finding himself unresponsive to the "powerful though vague and similar feelings excited by music." Darwin explicitly stated, "I retain some taste for fine scenery, but it does not cause me the exquisite delight which it formerly did." (See *Autobiography*, 91-92, 138.) Campbell's interpretation is an over-reaction against the overstatements made in Donald Fleming, "Charles Darwin, the Anaesthetic Man," *Victorian Studies* 4 (1961): 219-36.

[54]*Autobiography*, 139.

Darwin wrote Hooker after the latter had spoken of listening to Handel's *Messiah,* he said he would like to hear that work again, but added, "I dare say I should find my soul too dried up to appreciate it as in old days; and then I should feel very flat, for it is a horrid bore to feel as I constantly do, that I am a withered leaf for every subject except Science. It sometimes makes me hate Science."[55] The *Autobiography* records similar sentiments, lamenting that his former love of natural scenery, painting, poetry, music, and great literature had mostly vanished.[56] One pictures him withdrawn, like the only God he could begin to imagine. The world that he first found amazing and religiously sublime appears to have become, in his eyes, more and more perplexing, its mysteries increasingly opaque, its facts curious but less charged with significance. Even his science, eventually divorced from any keen sense of connection with the world of aesthetic pleasure, encompassing design, or divine purpose, began to seem less grand. In that atmosphere his theism was unlikely to thrive. That it survived enough to temper his agnosticism and occasionally to give him pause was surely not a sign of any resolution of the bewildering questions he had long habitually avoided. Rather, it signaled that a "quiet war" now and again still flared within himself, momentarily disturbing his mind's concentration and its cautiously guarded calm.

[55]*LLD,* 2:273.
[56]*Autobiography,* 138-39.

CHAPTER 6

EPILOGUE: RELIGION, SCIENCE, AND THE DARWINIAN REVOLUTION

Near the conclusion of his book on Darwin's life and thought, L. Robert Stevens observes:

> Darwin's work abides as a profound statement of the truth that science touches whatever is human. He saw this himself and considered long and carefully how his view would touch theories of morality, of art, of culture—the very heart of the human experience. If he is sometimes simple in his approach to these questions, he is also sometimes profound, and his bringing them within the purview of science by means of a biological empiricism is nothing less than a revolution in the history of ideas.[1]

Our study of Darwin's religious views and their connection with his science surely supports this claim. Yet it is important to remember that the revolution Stevens refers to—the revolution we sometimes call ''Darwinian''—actually had many causes, was exceedingly complex in effects, and was not always well understood by Darwin himself, especially as it affected areas outside of natural science per se. For this reason our survey of Darwin's informal theology and its evolution can perhaps best be concluded by briefly considering how Darwin's own reflections related to developments within the larger cultural context and then by highlighting certain significant features of the impact of the Darwinian revolution on the theology and religion of people other than Darwin himself. The particular question with which we will be most

---

[1]L. Robert Stevens, *Charles Darwin* (Boston: G. K. Hall, Twayne Publishers, 1978) 127.

concerned is this: How did Darwin's ideas both *reflect* and *affect* relations between religion and science?

That there were considerable tensions between religion and science in the nineteenth century is common knowledge. These tensions did not begin with Darwin, however, nor did their intensity in the nineteenth century derive solely from developments within natural science itself. Sir Peter Medawar is thus mistaken in his recent claim that, when T. H. Huxley sharply rebuked Bishop Samuel Wilberforce at a historic 1860 meeting of the British Association for the Advancement of Science, he "inaugurated, single-handedly, the tension between religion and science."[2] In point of fact, science came into conflict with traditional religious concepts of the cosmos almost the moment that pre-Socratic "natural philosophers" began engaging in cosmological speculations in the sixth century B.C.E. For many centuries the conflict was only intermittent. But with the rise of modern science, the potential for rivalry grew. Copernicus, Galileo, Newton, and later, a number of Enlightenment scientists all put forward ideas that to one degree or another conflicted with traditional Christian and Jewish teachings. During the eighteenth century, moreover, Kant's "critical philosophy" did much to turn the eyes of continental philosophers and theologians away from the heavens and the earth to the moral world "within." Although natural theologies and theologies of nature thrived in English-speaking countries well into the nineteenth century, they gradually (and largely unintentionally) began to pose a threat to traditional religious beliefs and institutions. While the conclusions of natural theologies and of the science they promoted tended all along to harmonize with commonly accepted interpretations of the Bible, research into the natural "Book of God's Works" more and more came to *guide* educated interpretations of the "Book of God's Word" and hence of scriptural passages such as those dealing with the creation.[3] As a result, the main locus of publicly recognized authority slowly shifted from the Scriptures and the church to natural science and its increasingly professional representatives.

The tensions between science and religion in Darwin's day were further heightened by the growth of historical science and the spread of the scientific historical study of biblical texts—the so-called "higher criticism."[4] Indeed, the publication of *Essays and Reviews* (1860), in which Benjamin Jowett's

---

[2]Peter Medawar, "The Evidences of Evolution," in *Darwin's Legacy,* Nobel Conference XVIII, ed. Charles L. Hamrum (San Francisco: Harper & Row, 1983) 46.

[3]Sir Francis Bacon (1561-1626) was the first thinker to emphasize the idea of the "two books." For a discussion of the importance of this concept, see James R. Moore, "Geologists and Interpreters of Genesis in the Nineteenth Century," in *God and Nature: Historical Essays on the Encounter Between Christianity and Science,* ed. David C. Lindberg and Ronald L. Numbers, (Berkeley: University of California Press, 1986) 322-23. This volume as a whole provides thorough documentation and analysis of many other historical points summarized here.

[4]In England the debate over "higher criticism" began in earnest with the translation of D. F. Strauss's *Life of Jesus* in 1846.

contribution advocated that the Bible be interpreted according to critical methods applicable to any other book, created a greater furor than that which followed the publication of *The Origin of Species*.

The controversies surrounding these two books were not unrelated; a major issue in both instances was the inspiration and authority of the Bible. In both cases the intensity of the controversy was due in part to anxieties that had been awakened long before. As Walter Houghton observes:

> To read an article like "On Tendencies towards the Subversion of Faith," written in 1848, and to discover that the author deals only with German rationalism and biblical criticism and is not aware of Lyell or Mill's *Logic* or *The Vestiges of Creation*, let alone such future bombshells as *The Origin of Species* . . . is to realize how terribly exposed the Victorians were to a constant succession of shattering developments.[5]

In this light one sees why Darwin's theories had such a disturbing impact. At the same time, one is reminded that Darwin's own crisis of belief was not atypical among thoughtful Victorians and that his rejection of biblical authority in favor of science was very much a part of an increasingly widespread tendency (visible even earlier in Germany) to subject scriptural texts to criteria derived from the historical and natural sciences.

Yet, having stressed the periodic tensions between religion and science and the intensification of these tensions during the nineteenth century, we must be careful to avoid exaggerating the extent of the conflicts. Contrary to the stereotypical view we have inherited from the nineteenth century itself, science and religion were not then (or now) engaged in an incessant "warfare," with all the progressive and enlightened thinkers on one side of the battle and with benighted, reactionary, and credulous thinkers on the other. This image, although widely accepted, is oversimplified in at least two respects.[6]

In the first place, it suggests that all opposition to controversial theories such as Darwin's was unscientific and ignorant—a mere excuse to defend traditional religious beliefs. In truth, even liberal scientists like Lyell had reasons not to be quickly persuaded by Darwin's theory. Many were troubled by the fragmentary nature of the fossil record, by the survival of apparently "useless" traits, and by the lack of knowledge of the precise mechanism for variation even within species (the discovery of Mendel's work and genetics

---

[5]Walter Houghton, *The Victorian Frame of Mind, 1830-1870* (New Haven: Yale University Press, 1957) 67.

[6]A number of current historians are critical of the image and rhetoric of "warfare" when used broadly to characterize the relations between religion and science in various eras, including the Victorian. See, for example, James R. Moore, *The Post-Darwinian Controversies* (Chicago: University of Chicago Press, 1979) 19-122; most chapters in Lindberg and Numbers, ed., *God and Nature;* John Durant, "Darwinism and Divinity: A Century of Debate," in John Durant, ed., *Darwinism and Divinity: Essays on Evolution and Religious Beliefs* (Oxford: Basil Blackwell, 1985) and the introductory chapter to Tess Cosslett, ed., *Science and Religion in the Nineteenth Century* (Cambridge: Cambridge University Press, 1984).

being far in the future). During the 1860s, moreover, the future Lord Kelvin—using the best available physics—calculated that the earth was not nearly so old as uniformitarian geologists had believed and as Darwin's theory of evolution needed it to be.[7] Darwin himself was troubled by these problems. It therefore hardly seems reasonable to attribute ignorance to all those who, in combining these scientific objections with those of a religious and moral kind, remained unconvinced by Darwin's arguments.

The depiction of nineteenth-century religion and science as engaged in persistent "warfare" is simplistic in a second way, as examination of the religious response to Darwin's theories shows. From the popular "battle" picture one would never guess that, in actuality, large numbers of religious believers, both conservative and liberal, quickly adopted (and adapted to) much of what Darwin proposed in the area of science. Yet we know that, soon after the *Origin* was published, Darwin himself witnessed the American Presbyterian botanist Asa Gray leap to his defense with an article entitled "Natural Selection Not Inconsistent with Natural Theology."[8] Darwin likewise received early and welcome support from Charles Kingsley, the eminent Anglican divine with distinctly liberal inclinations. It would appear that H. P. Liddon, a canon of St. Paul's, already spoke for a number of Christians when he said, in 1871, that evolution "from a Theistic point of view, is merely our way of describing what we can observe of God's continuous action upon the physical world."[9]

The ways in which evolution came to be accepted by various religious groups and individuals naturally differed. The Catholic Church, which had once been so troubled by the heliocentric theory of the universe, was somewhat less disturbed than Protestants were by the theory of evolution—perhaps because Catholicism relied less heavily on the authority of the Bible alone, which the theory seemed to challenge.[10] Pope Pius IX did issue the "Syllabus of Errors" in 1864, which condemned "progress, liberalism, and modern civilization." But while this list of "errors" was doubtless intended to cover Darwinism, its ambiguity actually allowed some latitude for speculation regarding evolution.[11] In the 1870s and 1880s, St. George Mivart, for one, was praised in the Catholic press for advocating a form of evolution in which the human body was regarded as a product of natural selection assisted

---

[7]See Peter J. Bowler, "Evolution: The Scientific Debate," in his *Evolution: The History of an Idea* (Berkeley: University of California Press, 1984) 176-205. Kelvin's estimates of the earth's age could not be rejected conclusively until the radioactive dating techniques of the 1930s.

[8]*LLD*, 2:163.

[9]Quoted in Moore, *Post-Darwinian Controversies*, 90.

[10]See Jaroslav Pelikan, "Darwin's Legacy: Emanation, Evolution, and Development," in *Darwin's Legacy*, ed. Hamrum, 82.

[11]See Gertrude Himmelfarb, *Darwin and the Darwinian Revolution* (New York: Doubleday, Anchor Books, 1962) 395-96.

by divinely endowed "special powers and tendencies." (By contrast, Mivart saw the human soul as created exclusively by means of supernatural infusion.)[12] The evolutionary ideas of Mivart obviously departed from Darwin's at crucial points. But other Catholics would later go further in accepting the agency of natural selection itself, and at last the 1950 papal encyclical "Humani Generis" officially recognized the possible validity of evolutionary theories while insisting on the divine origin of the human soul.[13]

For their part, Protestants frequently met Darwin's ideas with bitter and open hostility.[14] Nevertheless, their overall response to evolutionary science was far from being a declaration of "war." Liberal Protestants in England and America were, as one might expect, inclined to welcome evolutionary thinking, even though they often minimized or ignored natural selection in favor of Idealist metaphysics and non-Darwinian visions of change and social progress. Evangelicals, as one might also expect, at first reacted negatively, believing that the inspiration and authority of the Bible were at stake, that God's creative role was compromised or forgotten in evolutionary thinking, and that the special status of humans as creatures made in the image of God could not be maintained by followers of Darwin. But a surprising number of evangelicals, including leading "protofundamentalists" of the late nineteenth century and early twentieth, found ways to reconcile evolution with Genesis and Christian faith.[15] This was at least partly because even conservative evangelicals at the time had been convinced by earlier controversies over geology and paleontology that, as one historian puts it, "the text of Genesis must be understood in a less rigorous way that would allow the earth and its inhabitants to change [in some fashion] over a vast period of time."[16]

---

[12]Mivart's view of the human soul resembled that of Alfred Russell Wallace in his later years. Mivart died in 1900, having recently been excommunicated because of his increasingly sharp criticisms of the Catholic Church's resistance to change and modern thought. See Moore, *Post-Darwinian Controversies*, 117-22.

[13]The Catholic response to evolutionary theories is discussed in H. W. Paul, *The Edge of Contingency: French Catholic Reaction to Scientific Change from Darwin to Duhem* (Gainesville FL: University Presses of Florida, 1979); and in Pietro Corsi and Paul J. Weindling, "Darwinism in Germany, France, and Italy," in *The Darwinian Heritage*, ed. David Kohn (Princeton: Princeton University Press, 1985) 683-729; esp. 708-11, 721-26. For discussion of evolution by modern Catholics themselves, see Walter Ong, ed., *Darwin's Vision and Christian Perspectives* (New York: Macmillan Co., 1960). For a summary of more recent Catholic (and Protestant) views, see Arthur Peacocke, "Biological Evolution and Christian Theology—Yesterday and Today," in *Darwinism and Divinity*, ed. Durant, 101-30.

[14]See Moore, *Post-Darwinian Controversies*, esp. 217-345. Cf. John Dillenberger, *Protestant Thought and Natural Science* (Garden City NY: Doubleday & Co., 1960) 217-51; and Richard H. Overman, *Evolution and the Christian Doctrine of Creation* (Philadelphia: Westminster Press, 1967) 69-116.

[15]See Moore, *Post-Darwinian Controversies*, 68-76.

[16]Bowler, *Evolution*, 206. It was not until the 1920s that opposition to evolution hardened among fundamentalists and became tied to a strict biblical literalism and correlative forms of

Meanwhile, representatives of the orthodox Protestant mainstream were among those most likely to accept without substantial modification Darwin's scientific theories, differing from Darwin himself primarily in their insistence that natural selection be seen as the purposive working out of God's will and plan.[17] In general it seems to be the case that "with but few exceptions the leading Christian thinkers in Great Britain and America came to terms quite readily with Darwinism and evolution."[18]

The varied and often favorable religious response to Darwin's theories did not go unnoticed by the Darwin family. It seems, moreover, that Charles's reaction to this response was puzzling to some of his relatives. Two years after Charles's death, his cousin Julia Wedgwood remarked in a letter to Charles's son Francis Darwin that, oddly enough, his father had been "far more sympathetic with religion when his books were considered wicked, by the religious world, than when (as was the case for some years before he died), the dignitaries of the Church were eager to pay him the highest honour."[19] It is interesting to set alongside this statement Charles's own assertion that, had he known "how much more liberal the world would become" in the course of his lifetime, he might have ventured to write more about the connections between religion and science.[20] Doubtless some of what he would have written would have been more openly critical of religion; yet the attempt to state his theological reflections more fully might have prompted him to take more careful note of current theological changes that were more sweeping and significant than he probably realized.

In any case, in an essay published in 1887, Darwin's friend and defender T. H. Huxley made it clear that he himself had seen a change in the attitude of theologians toward science. On this occasion Huxley referred to three sermons that seemed to "signalise a new departure in the course adopted by theology towards science, and to indicate the possibility of bringing about an honourable *modus vivendi* between the two." This he contrasted to the situation a quarter of a century before, when it was often his fate "to see the whole

---

creationism. See Moore, *Post-Darwinian Controversies,* 68-76. For an account of special creationism since the time of Darwin, and an account of the current creationist debate, see Ronald L. Numbers, "The Creationists," in Lindberg and Numbers, *God and Nature,* 391-423; and Langdon Gilkey, *Creationism on Trial: Evolution and God at Little Rock* (Minneapolis: Winston-Seabury Press, 1985).

[17]See Moore, *Post-Darwinian Controversies,* 299-345.

[18]Ibid., 92. Christians—both Catholic and Protestant—were in a somewhat different situation in continental Europe in the nineteenth century. In France and Germany, for instance, complex factors prevented Darwin's ideas—at least in their original form—from having much impact even on science until the twentieth century. See Overman, *Evolution and the Christian Doctrine,* 62-90.

[19]Quoted in Himmelfarb, *Darwinian Revolution,* 386.

[20]Ibid., quoted 383.

artillery of the pulpit brought to bear upon the doctrine of evolution and its supporters."[21]

Both religion and Darwinian science survived the conflicts that erupted between them in the nineteenth century. But no lasting and mutually satisfactory *modus vivendi* was imminent after all. Around the turn of the century, Darwinism experienced a temporary eclipse within the scientific community.[22] By the time it had recovered, logical positivism had begun to heighten the antagonism of philosophers of science and a number of other intellectuals toward metaphysics and religion. The theological climate had likewise changed. One result and symptom of that change was that Christian theology in many forms and for many decades abandoned its former interest in science and the world of nature.[23] Promoters of the social gospel concentrated on human welfare. Neoorthodox theology was chiefly concerned with a God beyond both nature and reason or with the existential stance of the individual. Evangelical religion stressed the personal experience of God as mediated not through nature but through the Bible and the spirit of the living Christ. Neo-Thomist and process thought endeavored to reintroduce (albeit in radically different ways) theological and teleologial concepts into the understanding of nature, but in doing so seemed either outmoded or irrelevant to the majority of leading scientists and religious scholars. Post-liberal theologies focused on the analysis of religious language itself. Radical theologies proclaimed the death of God. Theologies of hope anticipated an eschaton unimaginable to science. Liberation theologies initially struggled to lift the burdens of the op-

---

[21]Thomas H. Huxley, "An Episcopal Triology," in *Science and Christian Tradition: Essays* (New York: Greenwood Press, 1968) 126-59; quotations on 127, 128. Huxley's account is, as usual, more than a little ironic, but the shift that he noticed was real.

[22]See Bowler, *Evolution,* 233-65. In referring to a temporary eclipse of Darwinism and its subsequent recovery, I do not mean to imply that evolutionary theory—accepted by almost all biologists and geologists today—has not undergone significant modifications in recent decades or that Darwin is now viewed as having been "right" in every major respect. See Jacques Roger, "Darwinism Today," and William B. Provine, "Adaptation and Mechanisms of Evolution After Darwin: A Study in Persistent Controversies," in *Darwinian Heritage,* ed. Kohn, 825-66.

[23]The following brief theological overview is, of course, highly simplified; exceptions to its generalizations abound, especially among Anglican theologians and in the empirical and process theologies of the Whiteheadians and Teilhard de Chardin. Nevertheless, the general trend is one that is well documented in histories of modern religious thought. It should be stressed that the virtual divorce between religion and science described here has been promoted as much by scientists as by theologians. At a recent Nobel Conference on Darwin's legacy, panelists were asked by someone in the audience whether the theory of evolution rules out a belief in God the Creator or in any supernatural being. Sir Peter Medawar's response was that, as this is a matter of faith, "there can be no logical discussion of it. Empirical evidence [and science] does not bear upon it at all." Stephen Jay Gould concurred that belief in God and views about evolution occupy "entirely separate domains," and was supported in this judgment by Richard Leakey. In this case, all three scientists were interested in avoiding *conflict* between religion and science; but in so doing they also excluded any possibility of *conversation* between the "domains." See *Darwin's Legacy,* ed. Hamrum, 113-14.

pressed without as yet considering the liberation of nature. Most of these theologies accepted something similar to a Darwinian theory of evolution; but for most of them evolution and nature did not much matter—at least not in any notably positive sense.

It is striking, therefore, that evolution and the natural world have at the moment once more begun to be of genuine interest to many forms of Christian theology, including new varieties of some of the theologies listed above. Even the revival of creationism (whether seen as science or theology or both) is partly attributable to the desire to bring science and religion together in some significant way. This growing religious openness to science and the natural world is probably due in part—and ironically—to the waning of the sort of positivist science and naturalistic metaphysics to which Darwin's work contributed so much. It may also have to do with the ever more precarious state of nature and of the earth itself.

For whatever reason, one witnesses now a renewed theological concern for nature. One also witnesses tentative new attempts at natural theology—attempts that try to take into account questions and insights generated by the very Darwinian theories that were supposed to have closed the era of natural theologies once and for all. Whether any of these natural theologies and theologies of nature would have satisfied Darwin himself, we shall never know. That they have captured the attention of a number of scientists, theologians, and thoughtful individuals with diverse creeds and commitments is plain—and plainly points to a new state in the evolution of Darwin's influence on religious beliefs.[24]

---

[24]It is impossible to indicate here the wide range of books beginning once again to examine nature from a religious perspective or adumbrating some sort of natural theology. I can only suggest that, on a popular level, both impulses are present in such writings as those of Annie Dillard and, to a lesser extent, the essays of the late Loren Eiseley; clearly they are evident in much science fiction and film and in popular books endeavoring to blend Western physics with Eastern metaphysics. On a more academic level the renewal of process philosophy/theology and the proliferation of studies of the relations between science and religion are indicative at least of a convergence of interests between the scientific and the religious spheres. Last, I mention four books the titles of which—even apart from the contents—point in directions that others are going: H. Paul Santmire, *The Travail of Nature: The Ambiguous Ecological Promise of Christian Theology* (Philadelphia: Fortress Press, 1985); Stephen Toulmin, *The Return to Cosmology: Postmodern Science and the Theology of Nature* (Berkeley: University of California Press, 1982); A. R. Peacocke, *Creation and the World of Science* (Oxford: Oxford University Press, Clarendon Press, 1979); and Charles Birch and John B. Cobb, *The Liberation of Life: From the Cell to the Community* (Cambridge: Cambridge University Press, 1981).

INDEX OF NAMES